The People'

Chels

Feeling Blue

by

Neil Henderson

Peter O'Dowd - Chelsea, 1930s.

Copyright © Neil Henderson 1998

First published in 1998 by

The People's History
Suite 1
Byron House
Seaham Grange Business Park
Seaham
Co. Durham
SR7 0PW

ISBN 1 902527 12 7

Contents

Jim Kordas brings the 1998
European Cup Winners' Cup
back to Chelsea.

Acknowledgements

I would like to thank the following people for sharing with me their memories of Chelsea Football Club and supplying pictures and photographs for use within this book:

Nick Bennett, Jan Bettis, Scott Cheshire (author of *Chelsea – An Illustrated History*), Jacquie Clarke, Ron Coello, Roy Coello, Nick Davis, Stephen Fairclough, Nigel Falconer, Ross Falconer, Stan Falconer, Paul Fisher, Sue Hawkins, Nick Hines, Russell Hines, Andy Jackson, Andy Jacobs (Series Producer, Avalon Television's *Fantasy Football*), Barry Jones, Nick Jordan, Tim Lovejoy (Producer/Presenter, Sky Sports' *Soccer AM*), Jim McSweeney, Rob More, Linda Richmond, Jamie Roberts, Kevin Ryan, Peter Scherschel, Richard Sharp, Tony Sharp, Jochen Staudt, Daryl Woodward.

I would like to extend my thanks to Sky Sports (in particular, Jonathan Sim) for the use of photographs and to Karen Henderson and Lynnette Hurley for assistance with typing and proof reading.

Front cover photograph by Ron Coello.

Introduction

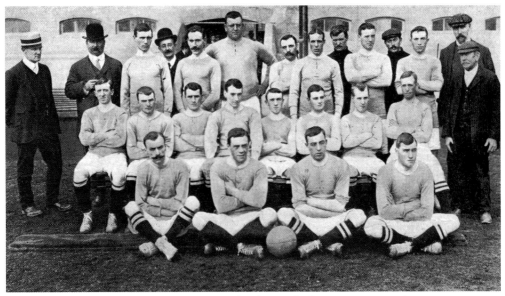

Where it all began – The first Chelsea team, 1905.

I first became aware of Chelsea in 1972. I remember the occasion vividly: I was four-years-old and playing Subbuteo on the landing with the kid from next door. He owned the Jules Rimet World Cup Edition and had an impressive collection of teams. England '66 and the Brazilian World Champions of 1970 sat before me, as did Don Revie's all-conquering Leeds United. I failed to recognise most of the teams, but I was mesmerised by all the colours.

My friend suggested that I choose my team first, which to the casual observer may appear akin to UEFA allowing the away team first call on colours in European competitions. My friend's offer, however, was not quite so generous and his gesture of goodwill was immediately trampled upon when I selected the 'little men in blue' – the only team, apparently, out of bounds.

Before I'd even finished gathering my first eleven, an angry finger had been waved in my face and I'd been told that I'd have to pick another team. Any team, in fact – except Chelsea. They were my friend's special team and reserved exclusively for his use. When I enquired as to why this was so, he proudly declared, as only one four-year-old to another could, 'Because Chelsea are class.'

I don't remember much about what happened after that, but I do recall nodding in pretend understanding of my friend's statement. Chelsea were class – of course they were. It made perfect sense that they be singled out for special treatment. Even to a four-year-old.

So that was my first experience of Chelsea Football Club. It obviously had a profound effect upon me because fast forward twenty-six years and I still find myself nodding in appreciation of those words. As I've argued in many a drunken football conversation over the years, the difference between Chelsea and their rivals, particularly their North London neighbours, is that Chelsea have always operated with a bit more swagger – a bit of class. Agreed, Tottenham and Arsenal have taken the lion's share of success in the capital over the last couple of decades, but Chelsea have continued to remain somewhat aloof – a cut above the rest. Even when the boys in blue failed to deliver on the pitch for near on thirty years, there was something about the club and its fans that kept the Chelsea ideal on a higher plane to the rest.

Put simply, there's something special about Chelsea: I know it, the fans know it and that kid in 1972 knew it.

When I set about writing this book, the idea was not to document the history of the club, but to depict what it means to follow Chelsea. To capture a little of the magic, if you like. To this end, I have spoken to many lifelong fans and some recent devotees of the club and they have shared with me their stories and recollections. I have applied the minimum of editing to each contribution, in order to remain faithful to the words of the story teller. Indeed, some of the stories included may not even be factually correct – time has a habit of clouding the memory. This, of course, should not detract from their personal importance. Finally, I have included as many photographs as possible from personal collections, to complete this 'people's history'.

This is the story of Chelsea Football Club as told by its fans. This is your story.

Neil Henderson,
London, 1998

The fans prepare to get their stories off their chests – Blues supporters, from left to right: Des, Flur, Eddie, Dan, Rob and Gary.

DO YOU REMEMBER YOUR FIRST TIME?

There are common milestones in all our lives; important events that shape and, with hindsight, allow us to plot the course of our days. Many people cite their first day at school as a turning point in their development. Then, much later, there's that first proper 'relationship'. But not all romances involve another person and that which at first appears to be little more than a passing fancy with eleven men and a ball, may well turn out to be one of the most enduring love-affairs of them all.

The true Chelsea supporter will never forget his first encounter with the team. He may not recall the facts and figures of that first game, but, like all great events in his life, he will carry the moment with him always.

Grab 'em when they're young! – Katie Davis.

Mayhem At The Turnstiles

The first game you go to should be an emotional experience. My first game was against Everton in 1957, when I was four-years-old, and I was totally captivated. Dave Hickson, the Everton centre-forward, was sent off. In those days, sendings off were much rarer than today and the whole thing just stuck in my mind. The next year, my dad got a season ticket for me and my brother. Being a kid I wanted to tear off the voucher myself and hand it in, but I dropped my season ticket at the turnstile. I remember my dad on his hands and knees trying to rescue my ticket, with people trampling on him. He was cursing me.

Andy Jacobs

Chelsea, 1958-59.

Chock-A-Block At The Bridge

I remember my first game quite vividly, because of the frightening atmosphere more than anything else. My dad took me in the 1950s when I was about ten or eleven. It was against Manchester United and we had tickets for the West Stand. I remember that the turnstiles were chock-a-block with people and it seemed to take ages to reach them. Half the time my feet weren't even touching the ground. When we did get in we found we had missed the first goal. Our seats were in the second row from the back, which is a hell of a way from the pitch when you're that age. It seemed miles away. And we had exactly the same problems getting out of the ground as well, with everyone leaving together. My feet didn't touch the ground from the time I left the ground until I got in the Fulham Road. It was quite frightening. We won 2-0.

Paul Fisher

Can't I Come?

My father had a season ticket for the old East Stand and used to go to Stamford Bridge regularly with a friend. I recall my father going out before lunch on a Saturday and coming home after the game and talking about it. I remember pleading, 'Can't I come? Can't I come?', although at the time I was probably too young to even read about football in the newspapers.

One day his normal partner couldn't go, so I was taken along. It was Boxing Day 1933 and Chelsea beat Sunderland 4-0. I don't recollect much about the match itself but I was very excited by the whole thing. I was hooked straight away and was very angry that my father couldn't take me every fortnight from then on. The following season I went to almost every home match. In fact, for the next five seasons, unless we were away on holiday, I never missed a game.

Scott Cheshire

William Mitchell – An Irish wing-half bought from Distillery in 1933-34 season.

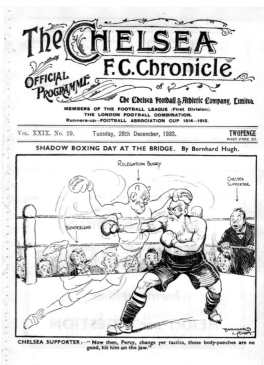

The programme from Scott Cheshire's first game, 26th December 1933.

9

Gordon Banks – Superman!

In 1965, we lost 2-0 to Leicester. They had Gordon Banks in goal and we had Terry Venables playing for us. I remember thinking that the players looked really huge. I wondered how Gordon Banks could dive and get that high off the ground. I was seven-years-old at the time.

Tony Sharp

Tony Sharp at Wembley Stadium, cheering on Chelsea in the FA Cup Final of 1997.

An Important Decision

My dad used to take me to various grounds in the early days: Charlton, QPR, Arsenal, to see different games. Those were the days when you could get hold of a Saturday newspaper, pick a game and just turn up and get in.

I finally chose Chelsea because most of the kids at school supported them. But once you've made that decision you're stuck with it. I always say that there're two things in life you can't change: your parents and your football team. You can change your job, your house, even your wife, but you can't change your football team.

Paul Fisher

Mother Knows Best

I used to go with my dad until he got a job and started working on Saturdays. I was eight at the time and started going to Stamford Bridge on my own. The first game was against Aston Villa and Chelsea won. It must have been 1966 or '67. That same year I had my first major row with my mother: she wouldn't let me go to see us play Manchester United with my mates, because she was worried I'd get hurt in such a big crowd. Chelsea were expecting 60,000 supporters for that game. My mother seemed to think that it was safe for an eight-year-old to go on his own in a crowd of 30,000 people, but not with his friends when the crowds were bigger.

Nigel Falconer

Green, Purple And Blue

My first game was away to Crystal Palace in 1969, which was the closest ground to my parents' house. My brother took me and we won 5-1. We took a bus to Selhurst Park and we had to get off a fair way from the ground because the traffic was so bad. The crowds were just enormous in those days. Someone lifted me up into the stand and I was taken aback by all the colour: the pitch seemed so green, the old Palace shirts were this marvellous purple colour and the blue of Chelsea seemed really bright.

The second game I went to was against Palace too, the same season, but this time in the cup. Me and my brother had gone shopping in Croydon, which was on the way to the game. We were walking back, past the ground, when a copper said, 'Got tickets for the game, boys?' We said, 'No, mister!' and he gave us a couple. We went in and watched the action, but we had to come away at half-time because mum didn't know where we were. She would have been really worried if we'd got home too late.

Nick Davis

Jackets And Ties

When I first started going in the 1930s, the crowd was colourless: no scarves or rosettes. Most of the men wore hats and there were very few women there at all. The whole thing was very sombre with most people on the terraces wearing jackets and ties. The noise, of course, was tremendous. But it wasn't chanting, it was cheering and shouting. There was a lot of applause and booing.

When we played away, I used to wait on street corners for the old classified editions of *The Star*, *Evening News* and *Standard* to come out, so that I could find out how Chelsea had done up north.

Scott Cheshire

Right: A star from the 1930s – George Mills.

Bovril And Horse-Manure

I went to see us play Blackburn in the 1964-65 season, when I was nine or ten. My dad took me. He'd been going for years and had seen the championship-winning side of 1955. The atmosphere was very non-threatening. No intimidation at all. There were young kids there unaccompanied. The crowd was huge. A poor crowd in those days would have been 30,000. I remember people wearing rosettes and swinging rattles. I remember the smells: Bovril and horse-manure from the police horses. Terry Venables and George Graham were playing for Chelsea. Of course, we had no idea then that they'd go on to become the celebrities they have. Chelsea won 5-1.

After that first match I was dying to go to another game. At the time, I would stay up to watch *Match Of The Day* in black and white – that was my diet of football. But it didn't compare to the colours and smells of going to a game. That first game was really good. It got me hooked.

As a small kid it was important that I got to stand right by the barrier, so that I was able to see. So my mum would cook lunch early and we'd get to the ground before two o'clock. For some games they'd shut the gates just after two because it was a full house. We never bought tickets in advance – you didn't do that then. It was first come, first served.

Jim McSweeney

Right: 'Ten Goal' Joe Payne – Bought from Luton in 1938 for £5,000. Joe gained his nickname after scoring ten goals for his former club against Bristol Rovers on 13th April 1936. He later referred to his feat as nothing more than 'Just one of those days'.

Choose Any Bike

In the 1940s, I used to cycle to Stamford Bridge from Battersea. Coming from the King's Road on to Fulham Road, there used to be a little row of cottages. They always had their doors open and you'd walk your bike in through the passage and into the backyard and park it. After the game, you could take any bike you liked, because nobody knew which bike was which. In all the years I was cycling to games, I never once heard of anyone losing a bike, or a bike being stolen.

Stan Falconer

Stan Falconer – A Chelsea supporter for over 50 years.

A Trip To The Opticians

It's strange how you recall important moments in your life through football. For instance, although I wear glasses now, I didn't always wear them as a kid. It first became apparent to my dad that I needed glasses when he realised I couldn't read the letters on the backs of the ball boys' tracksuits at Stamford Bridge. He said, 'Hmmm, better take you to the opticians.'

Andy Jacobs

London Calling

I was born and bred in Frankfurt, Germany and I'm an ardent supporter of Eintracht Frankfurt. In 1982, I went for an interview for a job working abroad for two to three years. At the time I was football mad and when the interviewer said that I'd have to work in London, it didn't register as London to me. It registered as Chelsea, Fulham, QPR, West Ham, Leyton Orient, Palace. I couldn't believe it and thought, 'Yeah, I can certainly go for working a few years over there!'

I got the job and the company rented a flat for me in Sloane Square, not far from Stamford Bridge. So, in a way, fate picked Chelsea to be my team. On the first evening after work in England, in November 1982, I walked down the King's Road to Stamford Bridge. A reserve game had just ended. The floodlights were still on and the gates were open. I walked into the ground and on to the pitch and had a look around. There was no one to stop me just walking in. The Shed was completely empty. I didn't take a dive on the turf because you didn't do that then. No, I just had a civilised walk around.

Peter Scherschel

A Dark Suit

I first went to The Bridge in 1968 and we lost 2-1 to Liverpool. Well, that's
what the record books say, but I could have sworn it was 3-1. Of course, I was
only six, so maybe I couldn't count very well! I don't remember much about
the match itself, but I do recall a man in a dark suit walking along the dog-
track in front of the Shed. The whole Shed spotted him and suddenly started
screaming, 'Enoch Powell! Enoch Powell!' My father thought that this was the
funniest thing he'd ever seen – I still don't know what was so funny about it.
As far as I know, the man in the dark suit wasn't the famous politician.
In those days they had crash-barriers on the terraces and I used to hang on to
one. At half-time I used to grab the coat-tails of my dad's coat and ask, 'Can we
go home now?' In fact, I sometimes still say that these days, to my brother.

Richard Sharp

Richard Sharp celebrates Chelsea's defeat of Wimbledon at Highbury in the FA
Cup semi-final of 1997.

I'd Rather Go Swimming

I was nine-years-old when I first went to Stamford Bridge. It was November
1963 and I went with a school friend and his dad. We were playing
Birmingham City. Neither me nor my friend wanted to go – we'd have rather
gone swimming. I was annoyed that my friend's dad had insisted on taking us.
Everyone around me was shouting for Chelsea, so I thought, 'Right, I'm going
to support Birmingham!' By the end of that season though, I was a devout
Chelsea fan.

When I started going regularly I used to go in the Shed with a couple of
friends. I lived within walking distance of the ground and it used to be two-
bob to get in. This was just within pocket money range.

Andy Jackson

Completely Chelsea

When I was young my dad used to make me sit and watch football. Chelsea were doing quite well then. A few kids in the street were Chelsea fans, so my dad went and bought me a Chelsea kit. Well, it was a Chelsea tracksuit and Chelsea t-shirt to be exact – not an official team strip. I was very excited by this and became 'completely Chelsea' from then on. I was three or four at the time. I didn't know anything about the team but I used to tell everyone that I supported Chelsea.

When I was older and started going to The Bridge with my mates, we used to catch the fast train to Marylebone. It would pull into the station and hundreds of Chelsea fans would get off and walk to the underground. It was a great scene. When we got to Stamford Bridge I was always really overcome by the atmosphere. My mates were older than me and would drag me along through the crowds to the turnstiles.

Tim Lovejoy

Gone To The Dogs

When I first started going to Stamford Bridge, there was no West Stand – there was nothing there. There was a dog-track around the turf, so you always felt like you were sitting thirty yards away from the pitch. They used to have speedway and dog-racing at The Bridge then.

In fact, my first memories of Stamford Bridge are of the dog-track. I used to go there with my dad, who was a big dog fan. I can't remember if I saw football or dogs there first, but if I think back to my early days, I remember the dogs more clearly. I guess its because it takes a while before kids understand what's really happening at a football match, but anyone can understand six dogs running around a track.

When I first started going with my mates, I used to go in the Shed. We used to get to the game at 12:30, when they opened the gates. We always stood in the same place, by the crash-barrier right behind the goal. It would probably look strange now to see a couple of eight-year-old kids standing in the same place before each game. But that's how it was in the '60s. Things seemed much safer. I didn't allow my own son to go on his own until he was thirteen. In fact, I can't imagine anyone in their right mind letting an eight-year-old go to a football match on his own these days. But it was no big deal then.

Nigel Falconer

STAMFORD BRIDGE STADIUM
GREYHOUND RACING
Every MONDAY and FRIDAY at 8 p.m.
and every
THURSDAY at 3.15 p.m.

Stamford Bridge has played host to greyhound racing several times in its history. Although dog fans remember best the meetings of the 1960s, races were also held in earlier decades, as this advert from 1933 shows.

A Famous Actress

As well as greyhounds at The Bridge, they also had motorcycle racing. They only had one or two meetings though, because the ground wasn't really big enough for speedway. The events were organised by some rich American bloke. I think he was going out with the actress Ava Gardner after her split from Frank Sinatra. Before the first race, Ava would parade around the track in an open-top car.

Actually, I once met Ava. I was a carpet-fitter and had a job down at Knightsbridge. In the flat next door was Ava Gardner, making me tea while I worked.

Stan Falconer

Ava Gardner.

Just Like TV

I first went to Stamford Bridge in September 1973, when I was thirteen. We were playing Wolves and the atmosphere was fantastic. When I got in the stadium I was really overawed by everything. I felt very emotional. In fact, I was so moved by the occasion that I was in tears. Just hearing the roar of the crowd and seeing the players in real life was amazing. I couldn't get over the fact that they looked exactly like they did on the telly.

Jacquie Clarke

The Lost Roll

I was quite a latecomer to supporting Chelsea. My family had moved to Wiltshire before I was born, so Chelsea weren't my local team. My older brother had been born near Wimbledon, though, and was a Chelsea fan. As I got older, I copied everything he did. So from 1968, I supported Chelsea to be like him. Of course, I wasn't old enough to go myself then – throughout the glory years of the '70s I followed Chelsea from afar. By the time I actually started going to Stamford Bridge, we were awful. I missed out on all the good bits.

When I did eventually go to a game, it lived up to all expectations. The atmosphere was brilliant and the action was really exciting. Even the fans were just as horrible as I had expected them to be.

My mother had insisted that my brother and I took a packed-lunch to that first game. She'd made us some rolls and we managed to eat all bar one before kick-off. As the crowd got bigger we dropped our remaining roll on the terrace. Just before the start of the game, Malcolm Allison, the opposing team's manager, came up to the Shed and taunted the fans. Suddenly, we saw our lost roll go flying through the air at him. It nearly knocked off his fedora!

Ron Coello

Jam Packed

There was a real buzz about Stamford Bridge when I first started going – a terrific atmosphere with lots going on. You'd walk down the street and see loads of police with their dogs. The first match I went to was in the Shed and it was absolutely brilliant, with lots of shouting and a fantastic atmosphere. I spent the whole match standing near the back wall, afraid I was going to be crushed.

Tim Lovejoy

Supporters celebrate as the final whistle blows on the last day of the Shed, 7th May 1994. After this last game, against Sheffield United, the old Shed was demolished and replaced with the new, modern South Stand (now known, affectionately, as the Shed End).

Huddersfield Away

I saw us play away to Huddersfield Town on 8th January 1983, in the third round of the FA Cup. At the time, Chelsea were third from bottom in the old Second Division. A German friend of mine came over to England and we drove up to Huddersfield with two other Chelsea fans I knew. The first thing that hit us about the north was that the beer was only 63p a pint – in London it was already 90p a pint. The second thing that struck us was that everything in Huddersfield was grey.

The game ended 1-1 and all in all it was a dire match. I couldn't believe Joey Jones, though: short sleeves in the middle of January, in the bleak north, showing off all his tattoos. He was running around in front of the crowd before the game, firing everyone up. The game was truly awful – I don't even remember who scored. I went to the replay, which Chelsea won 2-0.

Peter Scherschel

Favourite Shirts

I saw us play Sunderland in 1984 and I think we won 1-0. The atmosphere was just what I had expected – electric! I went in the Shed and it cost me about £1.50. The dog-track was around the pitch then, of course, and it looked like the stadium hadn't been modernised for about sixty years. I was nine or ten at the time and I've probably still got the shirt I wore. Over the years I've accumulated many strips, rosettes and tracksuits. I've never thrown anything away.

Jamie Roberts

Chelsea take on Sunderland at Roker Park in the '80s.

Kung-Fu Fighting

My first game was in 1976, when we played Crystal Palace in the fifth round of the FA Cup. Chelsea were in the Second Division then and Palace were top of the Third. It was 'the big game' at the time and the highlights were due to be shown on *Match Of The Day*. There must have been 54,000 at Stamford Bridge. I got there at one o'clock, two hours before kick-off and the crowds were enormous. There was a lot of pushing and I saw people fainting in the queue. One guy fell down in the turnstiles and broke his ribs. They had to take him out on a stretcher.

The game itself was amazing. Palace went 2-0 up and then, in the second half, Chelsea scored two great goals. Finally, Peter Taylor scored the winner for Palace. That was my first taste of disappointment with Chelsea.

That evening we watched the game on television. The only thing that Jimmy Hill was interested in was a kung-fu kick performed on a Palace supporter by a Chelsea fan. Some years later I found out who the Chelsea fan was. He was some guy from an estate in Putney. He's an old man now but his claim to fame is kung-fuing a Palace supporter on television.

Ron Coello

Ron Coello (front row, crouching, white jumper) and friends in Stockholm, for the European Cup Winners' Cup Final of 1998.

Home To Burnley

I'll never forget my first experience of Chelsea. It was the home game with Burnley in 1969. I was six-years-old and sat in the old North Stand with my mum and dad.

The traffic was tremendous that day, so my dad parked our car a couple of miles from the ground. We walked the rest of the way there and I was flabbergasted at the size of the crowds. The whole day seemed unreal to me because I didn't know what to expect in advance. This was in the days before we had a television so I had no preconceptions at all. My dad had already bought me a Chelsea kit though, even before that first game.

Barry Jones

Brotherly Persuasion

When I was younger I supported Manchester United. My mum and dad gave me a United shirt for my birthday. Then one day my brother came home from school and said, 'We're supporting Chelsea!' And that was it – I was a Chelsea supporter. I was easily persuaded in those days.

Nick Davis

Like Father Like Son

My dad used to take me to loads of different grounds when I was younger. He never made me support Chelsea, to be fair to him. But when I said, 'Dad, I want to go and watch Chelsea,' he was really happy. They were his team and his dad's before him.

Up until a couple of years ago my dad used to go to all Chelsea home games. He'd also travel to any away games this side of the Midlands. He's seen a lot, my dad – he was even at Wembley in 1967 when we lost to Tottenham.

He worked for *The Daily Express* and used to get press passes for the day. He's been to every Wembley final Chelsea have been involved in this side of the war. If you look at old television footage of great players like Jimmy Greaves scoring for Chelsea, you can probably see my dad sitting by the goal taking pictures for his newspaper.

Barry Jones

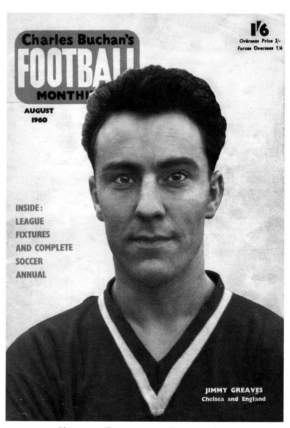

Jimmy Greaves – Cover star.

Greaves Debut

'… at White Hart Lane, where the 17-year-old Greaves, playing his first League match, saved Chelsea a point against the Spurs, Greaves may have a rich future.'

The Times, Monday 26th August 1957.

Sergeant Busby

The Second World War wreaked havoc with the early months of the 1939-40 season. Then, when things got organised, Chelsea played in the Football League South, as it was called. After the first few months, Chelsea would only have two or three of their own players, due to war commitments. They would have to turn out with guest players. They were always okay for goalkeepers because both Vic Woodley and John Jackson, the two great internationals of the '30s, were on war work in London. In fact, I believe Jackson probably played more as a guest for Brentford than he did for Chelsea.

Some fine stars turned out for us then. Matt Busby played for us once – Sergeant Busby, as he was then known. George Hardwick played for us for two or three seasons, as did John Harris. Harris was ultimately signed and went on to make four hundred appearances for Chelsea.

Those days were really exciting because you never quite knew who was going to play. The London newspapers were just eight pages long then. You were lucky if you got a couple of paragraphs on football on a Friday night – there was little chance of team news being printed. I used to stand by the tunnel at Stamford Bridge in those days. I'd hear messages being passed between the stewards: 'So-and-so hasn't arrived yet – I don't know what the manager's going to do!' The team changes used to come round on an old blackboard. Sometimes the names would go up and you wouldn't know who the players were.

There was a marvellous time at Watford when Chelsea literally had ten men. Word went round the ground asking for a volunteer and a soldier climbed down from behind the goal. He went off to get changed and played for us. He wasn't very good and Chelsea lost 1-0.

Scott Cheshire

Wartime 'keeper, Vic Woodley.

Who's Playing This Week?

Games during the war were strange because you never knew what type of team you'd be seeing. Any footballer in the Services and stationed in the south was free to play for any team he wanted to. In fact, I believe that when George Hardwick played for us, he was Middlesbrough and England captain at the time.

The atmosphere in those days was great. It used to take ages to get in because of the size of the crowds – there would be over 60,000 people there, week after week. If you didn't get to Stamford Bridge at two o'clock for a three o'clock match, you wouldn't be seeing the game. The gates would always be locked well before kick-off. Of course, everyone used to stand then. Us kids used to try and get a place by the half-way line so we would have the best view.

Stan Falconer

Joe Bambrick – A hero at The Bridge in the years leading up to the outbreak of the Second World War.

Stickers And Ticket Stubs

I once read in a magazine about a kid who supported Chelsea from a distance. He'd send off for programmes and sticker albums because he couldn't travel to games himself. When I first took an interest in Chelsea, I was completely besotted and did the same thing. I used to live out my support through these Chelsea stickers. When we won the FA Cup in 1970 I collected a whole album's worth of stickers. The funny thing is, I did a very similar thing when we won the cup in 1997. I collected the ticket stubs from all rounds of the cup. I even kept the tube ticket I bought for the journey to Wembley.

Ron Coello

Opposite page: Ron Coello's ticket stubs from 1997's successful FA Cup campaign.

FA CUP 4th ROUND
CONVERTED S.T.H
LIVERPOOL F.C.

EW HARDING STAN
14
X
121

CHELSEA FOOTBALL

LEICESTER CITY F.C.
CITY STADIUM, FILBERT STREET, LEICESTER LE2 7FL
24 hour Match Information: 0891 12 11 85
24 hour Ticket Information: 0891 12 10 28
Ticket Office: 0116 291 5232

PORTSMOUTH F.C.
P.A. WELD, Secretary
PORTSMOUTH FOOTBALL CLUB LIMITED
FRATTON PARK, PORTSMOUTH HANTS PO4 8RA
WHERE APPROPRIATE, THIS TICKET IS FOR THE SEAT STATED ONLY.
PLEASE TAKE UP YOUR POSITION AT LEAST 30 MINUTES PRIOR TO KICK-OFF

CUP 6TH ROUND
.F.C V CHELSEA/ OR LEICESTER
UN 09 MAR 1997 KICK OFF 01:30
NTER VIA APSLEY ROAD TUR

MILTON END BLO
ROW SEAT PRICE
X 41 £15.00
UNCOVERED SEATS RETAIN
MATCH INFO FOR
01705 750825

OODS FA CU
CONVERTED S.T.H
ST BROMWICH AL

THEW HARDING S

London Underground ⊖ London Unde

17 MAY 97 »1234«
. OFF-PEAK
01DAY TRAVELCARD
This side up • Not for resale
Issued subject to conditions - see over
This side up • Not for r
Issued subject to conditio

The Football Association Challenge Cup
SPONSORED BY
FA CUP
SPONSOR LITTLEWOODS

THE CUP FINAL TIE 1997

CHELSEA F.C.
TURNSTILE G
BLOCK ROW SEAT
147 24 120
KICK OFF 3.00PM - TURNSTILES 1.00PM
PLEASE TAKE YOUR SEATS BY 2.15PM
£45.00
TO BE RETAINED
6 869 070297 145817A

ARSENAL FO

"THE F.A. CU
WIMBLEDON V CHELSEA
SUN 13 APR 1997 12:0
NORTH BANK UPPER TIER
ROW SEAT PRICE
A 127 £38.00

CUP
EWOODS

CHELSEA FOOTBALL

LITTLEWOODS FA CUP
CONVERTED S.T.H
5TH ROUND REPLA

MATTHEW HARDING STAN
BLOCK 14

FA CUP SPONSORED BY LITTLEWOODS SEMI

The Delivery Boy

In the old days, the ground used to be packed with rivals supporters half an hour before kick-off. There would be a great atmosphere and lots of chanting. That's something you don't get now. The ground, of course, has improved since then. We used to be miles back from the pitch.

Back then I had a Saturday job as a delivery boy on my bike. I could quite easily afford to travel to the game, see the football and have something to eat. I doubt that a kid of thirteen or fourteen could afford to do that today.

Paul Fisher

A Foggy Day In West London

In 1945, Dynamo Moscow came over and played Chelsea, Arsenal and a couple of other teams on tour. We played them on a Wednesday and drew 3-3.

Tommy Lawton played for us and scored the third. It was a really foggy day and the field of play wasn't very clear. The crowd chanted, 'What's happening down the other end?' It was so foggy that at one point I swear we had fourteen players on the field. The referee couldn't see from one side to the other. That game was so popular that people climbed over the gates to get in. Kids were passed over the heads of older supporters and allowed to sit at the front. I reckon there must have been over 80,000 in there and we ended up sitting virtually on the touch-line.

A few international teams came to play at Stamford Bridge after the war. Chelsea had a bit of name for themselves at the time and were quite well-known around the world.

Stan Falconer

From Russia with lovely flowers – The Dynamo players walk on to the pitch clutching presents for their Chelsea hosts.

The Canadian national team playing at Stamford Bridge in the 1950s.

A Kiwi Conversion

Tromso in the Cup Winners' Cup, in the 1997-98 season, was the first game I saw at Stamford Bridge. The atmosphere was magic, absolutely brilliant! Electrifying! In fact, I haven't got enough adjectives to describe it. I really enjoyed it. I went with a few friends and we sat in the West Stand. Zola and Leboeuf were right in front of me, within touching distance – these wonderful players with such skill and such speed.

I'm from New Zealand and was brought up on rugby. My father used to say that footballers were just looking for an excuse to hug and kiss one another! At college we did have a football team, but they were very much in the shadow of the rugby players. When the first fifteen played, the whole college got the afternoon off to watch. But when the football team played, no one was bothered.

Before my first game at Stamford Bridge I felt much the same way about football. But, now I appreciate why people want to go every week. I'm almost tempted to get a season ticket myself.

Sue Hawkins

Sue Hawkins - Blue Kiwi.

25

Frank's Shop

When I was younger, Frank Blunstone, the old Chelsea winger, opened a sports shop. He was the first to sell replica kits via mail order. I sent off for one and it was the most exciting thing imaginable. I was eleven at the time.

I always wear a Chelsea shirt to games now. I've got 'Tore Andre Flo' on my back at the moment. There was a problem with the club shop at the start of the season when they ran out of certain letters. It was okay provided that you didn't mind being Gianfranco 'Ola' or Gianluca 'Ialli'! For my birthday, my kids bought me a long-sleeved shirt with 'Andy' on the back.

Andy Jacobs

Jimmy's Swansong

My first visit to Stamford Bridge was on 4th March 1961. We beat Birmingham City 3-2 and both Jimmy Greaves and Bobby Tambling scored for us. There were 40,000 there and we weren't even playing that well at the time. It was Greaves's last season and he later went on to score four goals against Nottingham Forest in his last game for us. I was really gutted after that season because I knew I wouldn't see him play for us again.

I was born in St Stephen's Hospital, Fulham Road, but grew up in Clapham. I used to go to Chelsea with my dad and brother and it was a really difficult journey from Clapham. We had to take the Number 137 bus to Sloane Square and then change to another bus along the King's Road. Then, in 1964, we moved to Battersea. This was one of the greatest thrills for me because Chelsea was now just across the bridge from my home.

Kevin Ryan

The Small Price Of A Striker

Jimmy Greaves had already scored a hat-trick in his last game when the referee awarded us a penalty. Greaves took it in front of the Shed End and scored. The referee then immediately blew for full time. So with his very last kick for Chelsea, Greaves scored. Then he was off to Italy for £80,000. It seemed a huge amount of money at the time, but you couldn't even buy the mascot for that price these days.

Stan Falconer

Hugs All Round!

Me and my mates used to go into Chelsea via Gate 13 and stand near the front of the terrace. If we ever got the chance, we'd run out on to the pitch and then straight back to the stand. It wasn't menacing at all – it was about trying to grab a Chelsea player and hug him. You would probably be banned if you tried that now.

Tim Lovejoy

Mascot Bobby Coello meets Gianluca Vialli – Or should that be 'Ialli'?

Five Goals Apiece

I can remember walking over Lambeth Bridge one day, listening to football on the radio. This was in the days before I'd been to a game. It was during the 1966-67 season and Chelsea were playing West Ham. The game ended five-all and I thought, 'Wow! What must it be like to go to a football match?'

Later that season, I got the opportunity to go and see us play Aston Villa. As I entered Stamford Bridge for the first time, I didn't know what to expect. I'd been to a lot of cricket matches, where you relied upon your binoculars to keep track of the action. I'd assumed football would be the same and was really struck by how close I was to the pitch. I couldn't believe how many people there were in the crowd around me. It all seemed unbelievable and I was in awe of everything.

We won the match 3-1. In fact, the first game I saw Chelsea lose was the 1967 FA Cup Final at Wembley.

Linda Richmond

Big Place, Small Kid

When I was still at school, I wasn't really too interested in football. My friends used to talk about it all the time and eventually I got to wondering what all the fuss was about. One day I decided to find out. I took a train up to London by myself and headed for Stamford Bridge. When I arrived at Fulham Broadway, I couldn't believe the number of people in the streets. It was all so amazing to me. I bought a ticket on the turnstile for the West Stand and made my way to the terrace. When I emerged on to the stand I was overawed by the enormity of it all. Now when I go, the ground and the crowds don't seem so big, but that first day it all seemed huge. Maybe it's because I was a lot smaller then.

Daryl Woodward

A Quid For Your Troubles

One of my earliest Chelsea memories is of Neil Shipperley scoring a really dodgy goal against Liverpool. It definitely did not go in but the referee gave a goal anyway. I was about nine-years-old and got bundled to the floor under a load of people celebrating. When everybody got off me, some bloke gave me a quid because he felt guilty about squashing a kid. I've been knocked over or shoved hard many times when we've scored, but that's the only time I've been given a quid.

Ross Falconer

SECTION TWO

THESE THINGS MADE ME WHAT I AM

Football has a habit of turning the world on its head. Supporting Chelsea can be uplifting one moment and then present us with the bitterest of pills to swallow the next. Less a game of two halves, more a game of two hearts: one swollen with pride and the other heavy with disappointment. How many of us have been down on our luck with precious little to look forward to, only for Chelsea to go and lift our spirits with one of those special performances from football's top drawer? Probably about the same number of us who've endured the misery of a crushing 1-0 defeat at the hands of lesser opposition, and then had the indignity of having to face smiling foes and adversaries in the school yard and workplace. No doubt about it, football has that unfathomable quality to both make and break us, and a lifetime's allegiance to Chelsea certainly takes its toll.

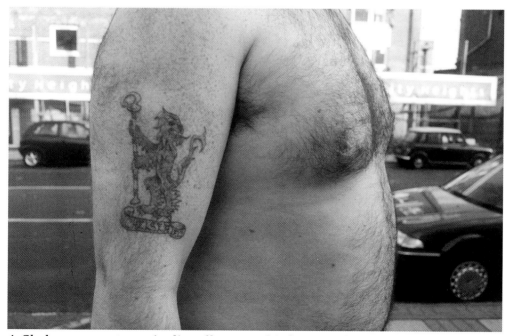

A Chelsea supporter quite literally wears his heart on his sleeve.

The Glowing Coat

One of the worst games I ever saw was when we played Manchester City in 1993. It was November and it was freezing cold. The game was being shown live on satellite television and the crowd was only about 10,000. The match finished 0-0 and, if my memory serves me right, City's Niall Quinn got a bad injury which put him out for six months. It was a truly bad game.

To make matters worse, for some reason I was wearing this awful coat – a real 'bad fashion statement'. It was sort of fluorescent orange/pink in colour. I'd bought it when I was holiday in America, even though it was the worst coat you'll ever see anywhere. Well, we'd video-taped the game and when we got home we sat down to watch it. Because there were so few people at The Bridge, every time a player ran down the wing the television camera picked out me in this coat. It seemed to be glowing in the dark.

Nigel Falconer

The Retaken Spot-Kick

We got slaughtered once at Watford. I think they might have beaten us 6-0. Johnny Bumstead took a penalty for us and missed. The referee said to retake it and he missed it again. Our friend Danny had had a lot to drink that day and the game was a blur to him. He swears to this day that the final score was 0-0.

Nick Davis

Nick Davis and friends resting in Spain before Chelsea's European Cup Winners' Cup tie with Real Betis in 1998.

Dreadlocks

My worst ever moment was when we lost to Manchester United in the FA Cup semi-final of 1996. I thought we were good enough to win the cup that year, but we ended up losing 2-1. In fact, for the best part of that game we were superb. When Gullit headed the first goal I let myself go and thought that we were going to Wembley. And as soon as I thought that, I knew I shouldn't have done it. Things on the pitch just fell apart immediately after. Thinking back now, I can still see Rudi's dreadlocks go up for the ball, and it's still a great feeling.

When we lose a game like that, I can't sleep for two or three days afterwards. I keep thinking about how close we were. I was devastated after that defeat. Really heartbroken.

Ron Coello

The teams line up at Wembley Stadium, with everything still to play for, before the FA Cup Final of 1994.

Too Much To Bear

The 1994 Cup Final was dreadful. I left my wife and some of my mates in a pub at Marylebone because they couldn't get tickets. I went back to meet them afterwards and I burst out crying.

Nick Davis

Keep Your Chin Up

There was a bloke sitting next to me at the '94 Final with his head in his hands bawling his eyes out. It's the only time I've seen a grown man cry. I said to him, 'Come on. I'm upset, you're upset, but we can't change the result. Let's go down the pub and have a drink and next time we'll win!'

Barry Jones

A Party In Sheffield

I've seen some awful games over the years but I think the greatest, most awful game, was on 31st October 1981. I was a student in Sheffield at the time. I chose to go to Sheffield University because I knew I could get to lots of other grounds easily from there – like Middlesbrough, Barnsley, Blackburn and Grimsby. Anyway, on this particular day we were playing away to nearby Rotherham in the old Second Division. I took the bus up there and we lost 6-0. We really hit rock-bottom. Petar Borota was in goal, our famous, maverick Yugoslavian, and he never put a foot right.

I went to a party in Sheffield that night and I drank a whole bottle of whisky. I was sick everywhere and some friends of mine had to clear it up. They didn't talk to me for a long time afterwards. It was just a terrible day, all in all – a day which just had to end with me getting drunk.

Richard Sharp

Mars Bars And Crisps

The Chelsea Independent Supporters Association used to run a father and son away trip once a year. We went to one at Liverpool. It was £10 for father and son, return journey. When you got on the coach, the kid got a fun pack with Mars Bars and crisps and fizzy drinks. The dads got to watch the 1970 Cup-winning video en route. It took about six hours to get up there and we lost, of course. Craig Burley scored a cracking own goal.

Nigel Falconer

Norwegian Pal

On one of my trips to Stamford Bridge, I met a Chelsea fan from Norway called Pal. He was already well known to my friends – when he entered the pub for a pre-match drink, everyone called out to him, 'Flonaldo! Flonaldo!' Pal is a Norwegian student at college in London and is Chelsea mad. His favourite player is Tore Andre Flo. After Flo scored against Brazil, when playing for Norway, Pal christened Flo 'the new Ronaldo' and had the name 'Flonaldo' printed on the back of his Chelsea shirt!

Nick Hines

Flonaldo! – Pal's legendary shirt.

Norwegian Pal.

An Away Day To Remember

In 1986 we went up to Aston Villa for a league game. We lost 3-1. These trips were always badly organised by a group of Chelsea supporters from Harrow. This trip had all their usual trademarks. The biggest mistake they made was in hiring a thirty-seater coach. When it arrived to pick us up, we realised that there were only ten of us. So we dived into the nearest pub and started ringing people to drum up support. We even offered to go round to people's houses to pick them up. There was one guy we knew who worked nearby. We went round to his office and literally dragged him out and said, 'Come on, you're coming with us!' It was madness and after all our efforts, we still only had thirteen people in this thirty-seater coach. We boarded it an hour late, after working out that it would cost each of us £15. At the time, you could have travelled on the special football train in style for much less money.

We got on to the M1 and eventually stopped at a service station. There were about thirty coaches in the car-park, all decked out in blue and white. We thought, 'Chelsea?' All thirteen of us walked into the cafe and then realised that we had encountered Portsmouth fans on an away trip. We walked in, used the loo, bought a few drinks, and then discreetly left. Then, suddenly, the Pompey fans realised we did not belong to them and ran out after us. They started chasing the bus! Luckily we reached the slip road before they reached us. How we got away I'll never know.

We continued on our journey and left the M6 about two stops before Birmingham – for a refreshment break! A couple of the guys had been to the Black Country many times and knew a pub with a friendly landlord. So, from one o'clock until a quarter to three, we were in this pub drinking. We eventually got to Villa Park at five past three. Unfortunately, by this time half the people on the bus were too drunk to watch football and so stayed onboard and slept through the game.

Peter Scherschel

Wedged Tight

We went to Barnsley in the FA Cup in 1989. We had a minibus and a couple of cars between us – a good turnout. We arrived a bit late so we ran from the car-park to the turnstiles. We were queuing to get in when the queue stopped suddenly. One of the lads, Simon, who is twenty-two stone, was in front of me. I said, 'Come on, Simon, hurry up! We'll miss the kick-off at this rate.' Simon replied, 'I can't get through!' Before I'd had a chance to take in what was happening, I heard a voice with a thick Barnsley accent: 'Come on lads, give your mate a shove!' Simon had got stuck in the turnstiles. He couldn't move – wedged tight, he was. So me and a few of the blokes behind started pushing. We got him in eventually but it took ages. We lost 4-0.

Barry Jones

Barry Jones taking it easy on a Chelsea away trip.

No Football!

In the 1980s we went to Bolton in a couple of minibuses. On the way back, we stopped off at some posh bar. As soon as we walked in, the manager said, 'No football!' One of us had his arm in a plaster cast. So somebody shouted out, 'That's alright, Peter's got a broken arm anyway – he's in no fit state to play!' Back on the motorway, some Tottenham supporters crashed into the back of our minibus. They'd been playing up at Coventry and we ended up giving them a lift.

Nick Davis

The Lights Go Out

In the 1968-69 season, we played Preston North End in the FA Cup. We were 2-0 up when, in the seventy-seventh minute, the floodlights gave up. Apparently, there was a fire in the main electrical junction box. The game had to be abandoned.

It was decided that the game be replayed during the following week, early afternoon. Of course, me and my mates would be at school then, but still wanted to go to the game. The teachers were wise to this. On the day of the game they positioned prefects all around the obvious sneaking out spots. A load of us managed to bunk off anyway and get to the game.

The crowd that day was about 38,000, which is not bad for a mid-afternoon kick-off. I think it was made up of 27,000 school kids, mind you! The game itself was unbelievable. We were losing with time running out and managed to score an equaliser just about on full-time. Then, two minutes into injury time, we scored the winner.

Nigel Falconer

Jim McSweeney – Another fan who was at the famous Preston North End games. He recalls, 'All the kids at my school bunked off for the replay – the teachers were livid.'

Promotion Celebrations

In the 1983-84 season we beat Leeds 5-0 and got promoted. I came running down from the West Stand, to try and get on the pitch to celebrate. It was absolutely fantastic. The stewards and police tried to stop us but there were too many people. I remember someone saying at the time, 'If this is what it's like going up to the First Division, imagine what it would feel like to win the title.' The scenes at Fulham Broadway that day were beautiful – it was just a beautiful moment. All the supporting you've done over the years seems worthwhile at times like that.

Tim Lovejoy

Picnic

When we beat Leeds United 5-0 to win promotion, I went with my sister, who was about thirteen, and a guy I knew from work with his girlfriend. We were standing down the Shed End when the girl who was with us brought out from her bag some sandwiches, a bottle of wine and a quiche. She proceeded to have a sort of picnic while the game was going on. My sister and I were both amazed and embarrassed by all this. Meanwhile, the Leeds supporters were going mad and trying to destroy our scoreboard! That was a surreal game.

Nigel Falconer

Football Crazy

My friend sent me this card when I wasn't feeling too great. It said 'Football crazy!' on it, and contained a little poem that went: 'Football is your passion, you give it your all, the true romance in your life, is eleven men and a ball!' That just about sums me up.

Linda Richmond

"FAIRY ON THE WING."

Of all left wingers of to-day,
  Our Fairgray is the king,
For graceful as a fairy
  Is our "Fairy on the Wing."

Glides along the touch-line lightly,
  Every movement light and airy,
Lithe and active, small but speedy,
  This is why we call him "Fairy."

Where with Chelsea lads he's honoured,
  In that Royal Blue array,
There his name has been converted
  By supporters to "Fairplay."

He is fearless of the charges
  Of the heaviest of backs,
As he darts along the touch-line,
  Helping well in the attacks.

Backs may rush to intercept him,
  But he's tricky as he's fast,
'Ere they realize their error,
  "Fairy" quickly dodges past.

As the thronging crowds behold **him**,
  One and all his praises sing,
For as graceful as a fairy
  Is our "Fairy on the Wing."

CONSTANCE M. P. JESSOP, Willesden.

Poetry and football have often gone hand-in-hand, as this pre-World War One cartoon of Norman Fairgray illustrates!

Lowest Points Ever

There was a great game in the 1978, when I was sixteen. I was in the Shed that day to see us beat Bolton Wanderers 4-3. With a quarter of an hour to go, we were losing 3-1. We stuck Clive Walker on and he scored a great goal and started the fight back. That was a truly amazing game.

That season, we amassed our lowest points total ever in the First Division. We were seriously rubbish and ended up being beaten by anyone and everyone. But managing to come back from 3-1 down and win was a little chink of light in the darkness.

Richard Sharp

Souvenir Turf

In the last game of the 1976-77 season, Ray Wilkins had the best game I'd ever seen him play. We were already promoted and there were 44,000 at The Bridge. We were playing Hull City and every time we scored people ran on the pitch. At 4-0 I ran across from the Shed up to the North Bank, past a group of girls. I noticed them laughing and suddenly realised that my fly had been undone for the whole game.

After the match I took a piece of the Stamford Bridge turf back home to Wiltshire. It went brown after three days.

Ron Coello

From Elation To Disappointment

You could say that football fans are a bit inadequate because they invest so much emotion into something they can't control. Like many fans, I've even gone to the lengths of wearing the same lucky clothes to each game. I think that in doing so, I can control fate and make Chelsea win. Which I know is ridiculous – but I do it anyway.

Of course, there are definitely times when even I realise it's all out of my control. Take that night in 1992 when Sunderland beat Chelsea in a cup replay. I watched that game on television with my friend, David Baddiel. We were depressed for most of the game, as Sunderland led 1-0. Then, right near the end, Dennis Wise equalised and we were overjoyed. Then Sunderland went and scored a winner and our elation turned to disappointment. Unbelievable. Actually, the first game of that tie sticks in my mind. Chelsea had led for most of the game when Sunderland equalised near the end. I was so upset that I allowed my kids to swear on the way home for the very first time.

Andy Jacobs

Andy Townsend – Chelsea captain for those titanic cup ties against Sunderland in 1992.

An Ideal Husband

I met my first husband on the terraces in 1969. When we split up, my next husband was attracted to me because I liked football. He was a Portsmouth supporter but used to come and watch Chelsea with me. When we split up, I started going with friends I met through supporting. All this probably sounds like a potted history of my life through football. Chelsea's got a lot to answer for!

Football, in some ways, is my substitute for comfort, relationships and friends. It's meant all sorts of different things to me over the years. When I got divorced for the second time, in 1988, I really threw myself into football. I ended up going to 98 percent of all home and away games and it was a great season for me. We walked away with the Second Division title by seventeen points. We even had a stunning 7-0 result against Walsall. I saw some really great games that year and football was a real comfort. Chelsea was almost like a new husband. It was get rid of one and gain another.

Linda Richmond

Linda Richmond and friends outside Wembley Stadium, before the FA Cup Final of 1994.

Ultimatum

My husband was a West Ham supporter when I met him but he supports Chelsea now. It was a case of marry me and marry my team.

Jacquie Clarke

A Horse On The Pitch

In 1985, Chelsea played Sunderland in the League Cup semi-final. In the second leg at The Bridge, I was sat in the East Stand. As kick-off approached there were still hundreds of people queuing up outside. They must have missed the start.

Chelsea scored early on and were murdering Sunderland. Then, Clive Walker, who we had sold to Sunderland, went and scored for them. Sunderland scored again and then all hell broke loose. People were ripping up their seats in frustration and some fans ran on the pitch. At one point there was a police-horse in the penalty area trying to restore calm. I thought, 'They'll have to stop it now, there's a horse on the pitch!' But the referee was having none of that. Sunderland broke away and booted the ball out to Walker. He flew down the wing, cut inside the police-horse and rifled the ball in the net. I couldn't believe that the referee allowed the goal to stand.

Nigel Falconer

Desperation

I'll never forget that second leg against Sunderland at The Bridge. A fat man ran on the pitch and tried to grab Clive Walker – it was an act of sheer desperation. I think Joey Jones intervened.

Richard Sharp

Chelsea take on their 'bogey side', Sunderland, in a 1913 encounter. Clive Walker was injured at the time and so could turn out for neither the Blues nor the Red And Whites!

Train Journey From Hell

Sunderland in the 1985 League Cup semi-final was terrible. I went to the away leg at Roker Park and the journey home was awful. We'd lost the game 2-0, so I was in poor spirits anyway, but then the train back to Kings Cross decided to break down five times. I ended up having to get off at Finsbury Park at four in the morning and take a cab back to South London. And even before the train had broken down, I'd ended up in the only carriage without heating. It was about minus four degrees in there!

Ron Coello

A Throbbing Hand

My worst ever football match was when I'd badly damaged a tendon in my finger. My mates came round and said, 'We've got tickets for you for the game down at Southampton.' I'd only had an operation on my finger the previous week and my hand was all bandaged, but I went anyway. About a mile outside Southampton they said to me, 'By the way, Tim, we haven't actually got a ticket for you, but we'll get one off a tout!' We stood outside the ground trying to get a ticket and the police put a huge ring around all the Chelsea fans. We weren't allowed to move. So I was out there in December, in the freezing cold, with a throbbing hand, for what seemed like hours. I managed to get in to the game for the last ten minutes, when they opened all the gates. It was the first time I'd been down to The Dell. I remember sitting on the pavement thinking, 'I'm freezing, I don't want to be here and I hate my mates for taking me without a ticket.' That episode aside, supporting Chelsea's normally a good laugh.

Tim Lovejoy

Tim Lovejoy in happier times, savouring Chelsea's League Cup success of 1998.

Guests Of Honour

A friend and I used to sit on the benches in the West Stand. Regular as clockwork, we would get there at one o'clock to get our particular seat on the back bench. I got to know the guy manning the gate and one day he asked if we would like to be guests of the club for the day. This was about 1989, when Chelsea used to pick people at random and invite them into the Boardroom. Anyway, the following game was against Manchester United. We arrived at midday and were taken into the Boardroom. We had drinks with Ken Bates and the visiting Chairman, Martin Edwards. Bobby Charlton was there too. Then we had lunch and were taken to our seats. We got to sit where the Chelsea Pensioners sit and we were even given a rug to cover our knees. It was excellent. At half-time we went up to a hospitality suite and had tea and cakes – it was just a world apart from your average game.

After the match we went into the players' lounge and saw all the players and staff sauntering around having drinks. John Hollins was manager at the time and he came over to chat to us. Ken Bates was really hospitable too. We were treated really well and had a brilliant day out.

Linda Richmond

Stamford Bridge in the early 1900s – Before the time of John Hollins and even Ken Bates!

Bobby Loses His Head

There was a 5-5 draw with West Ham in the late 1960s. It was after England's World Cup glory and the thing that really sticks in my mind is an incident where the ball went over Bobby Moore's head. For some reason he actually jumped up and caught it with both hands. The crowd really gave him some stick because he was the World Cup skipper. He was supposed to be 'Mr Class' himself.

Jim McSweeney

The Chelsea Fashion Scene

When I started going to Chelsea I was a young man growing up. There was this massive social scene associated with Chelsea and I was swept up in it. Every Chelsea home game would involve a group of us hanging out in the King's Road first. Sometimes we'd to go to the trendy shops in Shepherds Bush looking for clothes. Actually, fashion was a big part of the Chelsea football scene. I remember a time when people would turn up to games draped in gold jewellery!

We'd always try and get into a pub before the match for a bit of a sing-song. Most of us were underage at the time. Then the idea was to get to the ground really early to savour the atmosphere and to watch everything build up. Supporting Chelsea was just a way of life to me back then. In fact, in my mid to late teens, Chelsea was my life.

Tim Lovejoy

RFC Bruges

One of the best games I ever saw was when we played Manchester City in the Cup Winners' Cup in 1971. They were the holders and we beat them 1-0 in the semi-final at Stamford Bridge. That whole competition was great for us. Earlier, we had beaten RFC Bruges in a great tie. We lost the first leg at their place 2-0. In the second leg at Stamford Bridge, it was 2-0 to Chelsea at full time. Then we went and scored two goals in the extra period.

Paul Fisher

Ken Bates, Ticket Seller

I went to Stamford Bridge one lunch-time to queue up for tickets for a cup replay. It was in the early '80s when Ken Bates was first in charge at Chelsea. When I got to the ground it was the usual story: one window open at the ticket office and the queue going all the way up to Fulham Broadway. People were getting really annoyed. Suddenly, Ken Bates appeared with a megaphone and said, 'Bear with me, I'll do something about this.' And fair play to him, he opened three windows instead of one. He even went as far as to serve tickets himself from behind one of the windows.

Nigel Falconer

The Doc

My fondest Chelsea memories are of the Tom Docherty era. Even today, I think Docherty is the best manager we've ever had. The players he brought through were tremendous: Venables, Tambling, Bridges, Bonetti. Docherty created a good climate and paved the way for managers like Dave Sexton to continue. When Docherty left in 1967, I wrote to the chairman, Charles Pratt, blaming him for getting rid of the manager. I got a letter back accusing me of being libellous and threatening legal action. He withdrew his threat to take me to court, though, when he discovered that I was only fifteen. I was just so gutted that 'The Doc' had left.

Kevin Ryan

Left: Tommy Docherty – 'The Doc'.

Kharine's Blunder

The game against Newcastle in the FA Cup in 1996 is one of my favourites. We played really well that day and I was on the edge of my seat. We'd already beaten them earlier in the season and were playing brilliantly. We were leading 1-0 when our 'keeper, Kharine, made a mistake right at the end and gifted them an equaliser. The whole ninety minutes of that game I was shaking with nervous excitement and then, at the final whistle, I was so disappointed. I just couldn't believe what had happened. I didn't really know how much of a gift we'd given them until after the game when I saw it again on television. I suppose though, with hindsight, the draw was worth it because we went on to beat them in a penalty shoot-out in the replay.

Daryl Woodward

Daryl Woodward.

Hugs And Kisses

The best game I've been to was probably when we beat Liverpool 4-2 in the cup in the 1996-97 season. We were 2-0 down at half-time. Then Mark Hughes came on and the Liverpool defence almost wet themselves. Hughes won us that game. I felt a bit embarrassed afterwards. I was in the West Stand and ended up kissing the bloke next to me when the third and fourth goals went in. It was definitely a game for kissing and hugging strangers. To be honest, I do enjoy those games where you hug people you don't know.

Richard Sharp

Our Cup

That Liverpool game was really something. At half-time when we were 2-0 down, so many people left the ground. When we scored our second goal, my twelve-year-old son looked at me and we both burst out crying. It was uncontrollable sobbing. We were just so overcome with emotion. It was the most unbelievable game I'd ever seen and after that victory I was sure it was going to be 'our cup'.

Jacquie Clarke

Vicenza

The second leg of the Cup Winners' Cup semi-final against Vicenza, in 1998, was very special. It was my seven-year-old son's first European game. His favourite player is Tore Andre Flo and he wears a Chelsea shirt with '9 Flo' on the back. I come from Germany and support both Stuttgart and Chelsea. I'm really proud that I've created a new Chelsea supporter in my son. I hope to turn him into a Stuttgart supporter too but at the moment he only talks about Chelsea. Maybe one day I'll apply for him to be a mascot, when his English has improved. Then again, as far as his accent goes, he's already ahead of some of the foreign Chelsea players – and maybe even Dennis Wise!

Jochen Staudt

A view from the terraces – The players celebrate their 3-1 victory over Vicenza in the European Cup Winners' Cup semi-final of 1998.

All My Dreams Come True

A rather surreal moment occurred a week after the FA Cup Final of 1997. My girlfriend and I were staying in a hotel on the Isle of White. I went for a walk alone on the beach and saw this figure coming towards me. It turned out to be Peter Osgood! It was a really strange experience. I said, 'Ossie!', and he went, 'Hello, mate, how are you doing?' I said, 'Sorry, I just had to stop you – I'm a Chelsea fan.' He asked, 'Were you at Wembley last week?'

This incident was made all the more amazing because I'd been waiting most of my life for three things to happen. I'd wanted the Labour Party to win an election, Chelsea to win the cup and had always hoped to meet Peter Osgood. And all my dreams had come true in the space of a couple of weeks.

There is a German word, 'shaudenfreude', which means taking pleasure from somebody else's misfortunes. In the past, that's all I could do as a Chelsea fan. We'd never win anything, so all I could do was enjoy watching Liverpool or Manchester United blow the championship. But winning the cup and meeting Peter Osgood really changed how I felt about football.

Ron Coello

Seamus O'Connell

There was a great game in the 1950s, when Seamus O'Connell was playing for us. He'd previously been playing amateur football for Bishop Auckland and in his first game for Chelsea, against Man United, he scored a hat-trick. We still lost that match 6-5.

Scott Cheshire

Right: Peter Brabrook – Came through the Chelsea Youth Scheme, making his debut as a teenager in the championship-winning side of 1955, playing alongside Seamus O'Connell. Unlike the established O'Connell, Brabrook did not receive a champions' medal.

Muted Celebrations

Once, coming back from Grimsby, the coach ran out of petrol. Chelsea had won the First Division Championship but we were stuck on the motorway and couldn't celebrate. We managed to get some petrol from somewhere but by the time we got home all the pubs were closed.

Nick Davis

A Great Memory

Great games always stick in the mind. I remember beating Fulham 5-3 when John Neal was manager. Pat Nevin danced around two players to score. He didn't even shoot, he just rolled the ball over the line. Gordon Davies got a hat-trick for Fulham but ended up on the losing side. It was a sunny day, down by the riverside and we'd had a good drink beforehand. It was a meaningless game but it's still a great memory.

Tony Sharp

A Call Of Nature

In 1991, we lost to Sheffield Wednesday in the semi-final of the League Cup. The second leg in Sheffield was a night match. Me and my friends decided to meet up at lunch-time in Hammersmith. The idea was to get on the North Circular and then make our way to Sheffield via the M1. Well, anyway, at four o'clock in the afternoon we were still in a pub in Hammersmith – we'd got a little carried away with our drinking! We eventually left early evening. The guy driving the car wasn't drinking but me and my other friend, Rick, were somewhat tipsy.

Twenty miles out of London, Rick suddenly decided that he needed to go to the loo. There were no service stations around so he took evasive action. There was an empty wine bottle in the car and he used that to answer his call of nature. I asked what we should do with this now half filled bottle and Rick said he'd pour it out the car window. That way we could use it again if caught short. He opened the window and proceeded to empty out the contents of the bottle. At that exact same moment, the wind rose and the whole lot blew back in my face. Just one of the unpleasant experiences I've endured when supporting Chelsea. That, to me, is true football dedication for you!

Ron Coello

What The 'Papers Say

In the 1940s, when I was fourteen and working full time, I would never miss a game at Chelsea. I'd see every reserve game and every junior game and always stand by the tunnel. I'd even watch other teams playing at The Bridge, which happened occasionally during the war years, when the ground was used for cup finals and other big games.

I can remember one great game when we played Wolves, who were the absolute top team at the time. There was a big sports writer with the *Daily Mirror* called Peter Wilson. He'd written in his column that Wolves would rip Chelsea apart. Anyway, it was one of those days when Chelsea just couldn't lose. We were annihilating Wolves 4-0, when there was a bloody great bang somewhere in the distance. Before we could work out what it was, someone shouted, 'Peter Wilson's shot himself!'

Stan Falconer

A programme from Aston Villa's match with Charlton Athletic, played at Stamford Bridge on 20th May 1944. The match was a play-off between the winners of the wartime North and South Cups, with gate receipts going to the King George's Fund For Sailors. 38,840 people turned up for the game, paying £6,947 in total to the charity.

The Adelphi

We never win at Liverpool. In fact, we always get hammered. Yet once in '92, I decided it would be good for all the family to go up to Liverpool to see us play. My wife came along and we stayed at The Adelphi Hotel. We made a real weekend of it. And blow me, Chelsea won! To be there on that day was tremendous.

Andy Jacobs

Don't Forget The Bad Times

People have a different perception of Chelsea now and always expect us to win. What they've got to remember is that we were awful for twenty years. The only reason we won the cup in 1997 was because I've served my time supporting us through twenty-odd years of thin and even thinner!

Nigel Falconer

WE COULD BE HEROES

Picture the scene: it's a huge game at The Bridge and the air of anticipation and expectancy is almost unbearable. The intro-music is playing loudly over the PA system and the skies are already awash with blue and white balloons and confetti, when the roar goes up to signal the arrival of the players from the tunnel. One by one, you sing their names, showing, in advance, your appreciation of the magic they are surely about to weave. And they, in return, raise their hands above their heads and applaud your efforts. So much excitement and passion, and all before a ball's even been kicked.

Now, close your eyes, rewind, and picture the scene again. Only this time, imagine that you're one of the elite eleven striding on to the pitch. How does it feel to hear the fans sing your name with all the passion that their hearts can muster, knowing that you have within yourself the power to break those same hearts in two? You may have kicked a ball a bit as a kid and convinced yourself that, given the right opportunities, you could be down there on the turf now. But the truth is that the great players, and I mean the truly great players, are a breed apart from you and I. Our loyalties and fervour for success may be just as strong as theirs, but they possess something more: the ability to make our dreams come true for us. And the best of all these players to pull on a blue shirt over the years – they become heroes

Jimmy Greaves – Hero.

Chelsea's First Hero

When Chelsea Football Club was founded in 1905, the chairman, Claude Kirby, appointed John Tait Robertson as player-manager. Robertson was a Scottish international half-back, with much experience of the game under his belt. With three Scottish championship medals and a Scottish FA Cup winners' medal to his name, he set upon the Stamford Bridge challenge with his usual gusto – assured in his belief that Chelsea FC were, 'destined to be the leading club of the metropolis'.

J.T. Robertson

Photo by Durrell & Martin, Tooting, S.W.] KEY-LIST OF PLAYERS (GIVING HEIGHTS & WEIGHTS) & OFFICIALS.

| MOIR (Assistant Trainer) | E. W. REILLY 5ft. 7½in.; 11st. 9½lb. | CANE 5ft. 8½in.; 11st. 13lb. | CARTWRIGHT 5ft. 10½in.; 12st. 11½lb. | CAMERON 5ft. 9in.; 12st. 12½lb. | KENNEDY 5ft. 9½in.; 11st. 1lb. | HARDING 5ft. 8in.; 11st. 7½lb. | RANSOM (Trainer) |
| MILLER 5ft. 5½in.; 12st. 1lb. | A. J. PALMER (Assistant Sec.) | D. CALDERHEAD (Sec.-Manager) | HENDERSON 5ft. 7in.; 11st. 10lb. | WARREN 5ft. 8½in.; 12st. 9½lb. | ROBINSON 5ft. 10½in.; 12st. 9½lb. | BRAWN 5ft. 2½in.; 13st. 5lb. | DOUGLAS 5ft. 8½in.; 11st. 2½lb. | DOLBY 5ft. 7½in.; 11st. 7½lb. | WHITLEY 6ft. 0½in.; 14st. 1lb. | BIRNIE 5ft. 11½in.; 12st. 8½lb. | M'KENZIE 5ft. 7½in.; 11st. 1lb. | KEY 5ft. 3½in.; 11st. 5lb. |

DIRECTORS: Messrs. G. SCHOMBERG, J. H. MALTBY, H. A. MEARS, W. C. KIRBY (Chairman), J. T. MEARS, F. W. PARKER, T. L. KINTON, AND E. H. JANES.

| WALTON 5ft. 8½in.; 12st. 9lb. | FREEMAN 5ft. 7½in.; 10st. 4½lb. | ROUSE 5ft. 11½in.; 12st. | HILSDON 5ft. 8½ n.; 12st. 2lb. | M'ROBERTS (Captain) 5ft. 9in.; 12st. | WINDRIDGE 5ft. 7in.; 11st. 1lb. | HUMPHREYS 5ft. 7½in.; 12st. | BRIDGEMAN 5ft. 6½in.; 11st. 8lb. | FAIRGRAY 5ft. 4½in.; 9st. 2½lb. |

Chelsea, 1908-09 – Robertson had by now been replaced by David Calderhead who arrived as manager in 1907 and remained in the role for twenty-six years.

Wartime Football

During the First World War, whilst serving in the Grenadier Guards, England international Charlie Buchan turned out as a guest player for Chelsea. He recalled his time at the Bridge in his autobiography *A Lifetime in Football*:

'It was a wartime League they were in, and that season Chelsea had a wonderful side. An outstanding player was the Danish international Nils Middleboe, the centre half.

He was over six feet and sparely-built. But it was wonderful what he could do with his long legs. He could use the ball accurately either with his head or feet.

Another great player in that side was little Bobby Thompson, the centre-forward. He had lost one eye through an accident when a boy, but it never worried him. He was so quick-thinking and fast that you could hardly believe he had not the sight of both eyes.

Thompson scored 40 goals that season and I bagged 39 ... In one game with Clapton Orient, at Millfield Road, I scored five of Chelsea's goals. But on the Sunday I was peeling potatoes on fatigue. I was not allowed to forget I was a soldier.'

Danish international Nils Middleboe, centre of front row, with his Chelsea team-mates.

The *Chelsea FC Chronicle* – The club's first matchday magazine

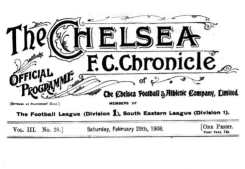

1908

1924

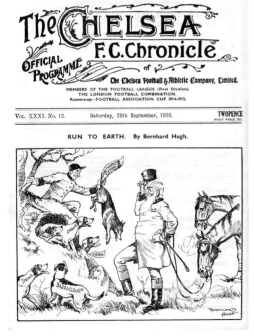

1935

1938

Hughie Gallacher.

Three Internationals

At one stage in the 1930s, Chelsea
had three international centre-
forwards on their books. The great
Hughie Gallacher was a volatile but
marvellous player. He was only five
foot six but had a real spring in his
heels. I remember him in a famous
match against Arsenal, when he
challenged their centre-half Herbie
Roberts, who was about six foot
two. I don't think he beat him in
the air but he was getting up as
high as him.

Another forward, George Gibson,
was as good a dribbler of the ball as
I've seen. Little Dick Spence was
another great player. He was a
Chelsea servant for thirty years and
lived down the King's Road to the
day he died.

Scott Cheshire

Right: Dick Spence.

Chelsea between the wars. Back row, left to right: Hutchinson, Priestley, Grey, Marsh, Hampton, Barrett, Linfoot, Bennett. Third row: Meehan, Dale, Harrison, Frew, Thain, Ferguson, Holling. Second row: Ford, Lee, Armstrong, Wilding, Howard-Baker, Sillito, Alsop, Langton, Smith. Front row: Haywood, Sharp, Ashford, Cock, Harrow, Cameron, Duncan, Smith, McNeil.

Ted Drake, Chelsea manager of the '50s.

Champions Thrashed

When Wolves visited Stamford Bridge at the start of the 1958-59 season they had high expectations as they were the reigning League champions. The young Chelsea team thrashed the star-studded Wolves side 6-2. Despite this early setback the champions went on to retain their title.

'Little Greaves, a harmless looking chap, scored five goals and had a sixth disallowed … They had no one to match the superb opportunism of Greaves … Next time, perhaps, Wright and company may think of some way to curb Chelsea's smallest forward; on Saturday's evidence a ball and chain seem the only answer.'

The Times,
Monday 1st September 1958.

A Brave Player

Osgood was great. You always look back fondly but even looking at clips of him in the cold light of day, he was an outstanding player. Another good player was Ian Hutchinson. He was very brave. Whenever the ball was in the opposition's final third, you always had a chance of scoring with Hutchinson on the pitch.

Paul Fisher

The Complete Footballer

Peter Osgood was the greatest player I ever saw. If he played today, he'd still be a tremendous player. He had skill, he had pace, he could shoot, he could pass. He was the complete footballer.

Andy Jacobs

The Sheepskin Coat

Once I was in a pub in the Fulham Road when in walked Peter Osgood. He was wearing the biggest sheepskin coat I've ever seen in my life. It must have cost the lives of five or six sheep!

Peter Scherschel

Still got the magic – Peter Osgood turns out for a charity match in the 1990s.

Vic Woodley

I would rate Vic Woodley and Peter Bonetti as the best 'keepers we've ever had. Woodley was perhaps the one player who kept Chelsea in the top flight throughout the 1930s and, if pressed, I would put him slightly ahead of Bonetti. He played the last seventeen internationals for England before the war and kept the great Frank Swift out of the side. I can remember going in the late '30s to many games and seeing Vic Woodley keep us in the match.

Another great goalkeeper was Harry Medhurst, from the '50s. He was only five foot nine tall and so didn't get the recognition he deserved. He was very, very good.

Scott Cheshire

Vic Woodley – The best 'keeper ever.

Frank Blunstone.

The Best Present Ever

When I was a kid I used to play in goal and Peter Bonetti was my hero. My dad took me to Frank Blunstone's sports shop on Lavender Hill and bought me a Peter Bonetti shirt and a Peter Bonetti pair of gloves. I was twelve or thirteen and it was the best present I'd ever had.

Nigel Falconer

A Great 'Keeper

When I was a kid, Osgood was the most acclaimed player. Peter Bonetti was a great 'keeper – probably the greatest we've had in my lifetime. The thing about Chelsea fans is that they know a great player when they see one.

Jim McSweeney

Stay Blue!

All the Chelsea players I've met still love Chelsea. We seem to be one of those teams that once you've played for, you stay loyal to. I met Peter Bonetti at Sky Television, where I work. As he left the television studio he said to me, 'Tim, stay blue!' I remember thinking, 'Brilliant! Peter Bonetti told me to stay blue!' You don't get much more famous a footballer than him.

Tim Lovejoy

Champion 'keepers

Although never achieving the domestic football success, with Chelsea, of latter day goalkeeper Bonetti, both Howard Baker and Brebner were champions in their own right – Howard Baker excelled at high-jumping, and Brebner went on to win the gold medal, when playing in Great Britain's football team at the 1912 Olympic Games in Stockholm.

Right: R.G. Brebner, gold medalist. There is an Olympic gold medal winner at The Bridge today. Full back Albert Ferrer, signed from Barcelona, helped Spain win the Olympic football title in 1992.

Below: B. Howard Baker, in international athletic vest and the Chelsea 'keeper's jersey.

Charlie Cooke

Charlie Cooke was a mesmerising player. You'd go to watch a football match just to see him play and you don't say that about many players. He was a great entertainer.

Once in the late '60s, I saw him play for Scotland against England and he single-handedly won the game for them.

Kevin Ryan

A Nice Guy

I got to know Ray Wilkins because he'd see my face at so many away games. He was a nice guy, very unassuming. Even after he'd broken into the first team, he'd still turn up to watch his older brother Graham play for the reserves.

Jacquie Clarke

Charlie Cooke – Mesmerising.

Kiss My Boots

When I was fifteen or sixteen I idolised Ray Wilkins. In 1977 we were playing Aston Villa at home and drawing 0-0. It was a really boring game, when suddenly, some fan climbed out of the West Stand and walked over to Ray Wilkins. The fan bent down and kissed Ray's boots and then walked off the pitch again. Of course, the stewards got him on the way off and he was thrown out of the ground. But that summed up how most Chelsea fans felt about Wilkins. He could pass a ball sixty yards

Ray Wilkins – '70s 'pop' star.

and it would fall at a striker's feet. He had such vision, it was incredible. He once scored from a corner against Leeds United. The ball just swung into the net. I've only ever seen that happen once. When we sold him to Manchester United I was gutted.

Richard Sharp

Sheer Class

Ray Wilkins was sheer class. I've taken so much stick defending that man. Even when he went to Manchester United, I stood up for that geezer.

Nick Davis

A Bit Of Panache

Ray Wilkins was the first player where I thought, 'Yeah, brilliant!' Chelsea went through a stage in the '80s where we had this dreadful run of results, but I still love Wilkins and a lot of players from that era. Joey Jones was great. Even though he had a Liverpool tattoo, he was committed to Chelsea. He would walk over to the East Stand and the Shed and shout, 'Come on!', and get everyone going. I used to love him for that.

    I also loved Clive Walker because he gave Chelsea a little bit of panache. He had these long flowing blonde locks and to this day, that image always reminds me of great times at Chelsea. I always thought we had great kits in those days too.

Tim Lovejoy

The Boomerang Shot

I remember an extraordinary day at Bolton once, where it was a dark Lancashire afternoon. Clive Walker hit this goal which curved like a boomerang into the top corner – no goalkeeper could have stopped it. That really saved Chelsea from going down into the Third Division. I've read that it was possibly the most important goal ever scored for Chelsea and I wouldn't argue with that. Walker was a great character.

Scott Cheshire

Clive Walker – Charming supporter Jacquie Clarke in the '70s with his 'flowing blonde locks' and playing for Sunderland in the '80s.

Headless Chicken

I really liked Clive Walker. The Chelsea team of 1976-77 won promotion from the old Second Division and we had Clive Walker and Steve Finnieston in it Steve Finnieston scored over 20 goals in that season. Eddie McCreadie was manager and we had a good side in those days. Clive Walker could do the one hundred metres in eleven seconds in football boots – he was very quick. Tommy Langley was playing for us as well, then. He was a bit of a headless chicken but scored some great goals.

Richard Sharp

Tommy Baldwin

I once met Tommy Baldwin, who was a Geordie playing for us in the late '60s. I was in a pub near the ground and he happened to be in there. I had a game of darts with him. He wasn't a bad darts player, actually.

Jim McSweeney

Alan Hudson

One of the last times I remember seeing Alan Hudson play for Chelsea was against Stoke in the 1970s. It was a midweek game and Gordon Banks was still playing for them. I'm 99.9 percent certain that as Alan Hudson was running out, he was smoking a cigarette, which he then discarded at the edge of the pitch. Even then, when attitudes were very different, I was absolutely shocked at seeing a player smoke. I remember that he scored a brilliant goal: he picked the ball up on the half-way line, beat two defenders and dribbled it round Gordon Banks. Absolutely stunning. All after he'd been smoking a fag. I guess it would have been the epitome of uncool, though, if he'd been smoking a pipe.

Nigel Falconer

Alan Hudson.

Tiny Strips

At a club dinner dance in the early '80s, every table had a Chelsea player on it. On our table was Colin Lee and his wife. We didn't really spend much time talking about football. It was more where you lived and what you did. He was a really nice guy and his wife was really sweet. I won one of the prizes in the raffle that night and had to go up on stage to collect it. It was a Chelsea football kit and the guy giving out the prizes said that I couldn't have it unless I modelled it. I went bright red and walked off with the strip feeling really silly. I didn't model it – I mean, it was when they had tight shirts and really small shorts that just about covered you.

Linda Richmond

Spackers!

My favourite player of all time? – I think I'd go for the unsung hero, Nigel Spackman. In 1989, I ran the London Marathon. I was being sponsored by a couple of charities and wrote to Chelsea asking if I could have an official shirt, signed by the players, to wear for the run. The club obliged, sending me Spackman's number six shirt. It was the old yellow away kit. They didn't have names on them then, so it didn't say 'Spackers' on the back. Unfortunately, I had to return the shirt afterwards. Nigel Spackman always gave his best.

Peter Scherschel

Peter Scherschel tackles the London Marathon disguised as Nigel Spackman.

Kerry Gold!

I loved Kerry Dixon – he was the best for me, definitely. I think the ultimate in his career was when he scored twice for England against the Germans, on a tour of the USA. He was the bees-knees for us at the time. He was the top striker in the country and he played for Chelsea.

If Dixon had had the right team-mates around him he would have looked even better. If he was in the current Chelsea team he'd still be a great asset. He was lightening quick and a natural goalscorer.

Jamie Roberts

Pat Nevin – Ace Dribbler

Pat Nevin is my favourite player ever. He used to come on the pitch to warm up and juggle the ball. In a game against Newcastle in 1984, Nevin picked up a loose ball on the edge of our area. He dribbled down the left and I'd swear he took the ball past twelve players. He dribbled past some players twice. He got right to the by-line, in Newcastle's six yard box, and knocked the ball across the goal. Dixon came flying in and just failed to connect. It would have been the goal of anyone's lifetime. Nevin was a throw-back to the old style wingers. He was full of skill.

Barry Jones

Super Skills

One of the most amazing things I ever saw was when I went up to Leicester for a night game. Steve Lynex was marking Pat Nevin. Nevin got the ball and didn't nutmeg Lynex, but actually danced around the player with the ball. Steve Lynex turned to the Chelsea fans with his arms stretched out in front of him, as if to say, 'What am I supposed to do?' All the Chelsea fans applauded him. It was one of those incredible moments between player and fans.

Richard Sharp

Post-Punk-Rock Footballer

I used to be a big fan of Pat Nevin. He wasn't your typical sportsman – he was well-read and interested in popular music. He was a sort of post-punk-rock footballer. They did an article on him in the *New Musical Express*, which I kept on my bedroom wall. Once, I was coming down the King's Road when I met him and we had a little chat. He was great.

I met him another time at a get-together for club-members in 1984. There were three players there as guest speakers: Doug Rougvie, Gordon Davies and Dale Jasper. After about four hours, Nevin turned up and drifted in. I said, 'Pat, would you like a drink?' This was shortly after the *NME* interview, so I told him I liked the article and asked if I could take his picture. He obliged and we had a great chat – he was a lovely bloke. Right up until the time he left the club, I still thought that he was 'the man'. He was gifted as a footballer and academically clever. Then he went to Everton and that destroyed him for me. I lost all faith in him after that.

Ron Coello

A Real Cool Bloke

I always liked Pat Nevin. One, because he was skilful, and two, because he knew a lot about music. He was a real cool bloke. The *Daily Mirror* once did an interview with him about his love of music and films. He wore a 1940s fedora for the interview. The other players would be into Rod Stewart and Nevin would turn up with tapes from trendy bands like New Order. He would try and persuade the other players to go to gigs with him. Apparently once, he was in the players' bar after a game, when a supporter came up to him to with a handful of bootlegs by the band Joy Division. The supporter said to him, 'I don't know anything about these, but my son says I'm to give them to you!' I was behind Nevin once in a queue outside a Chelsea cinema. I was going to see a German film. I didn't speak to him though – I'm no good with celebrities.

Tony Sharp

Pat Nevin appears in the
Daily Mirror, Friday 7th December
1984 – wearing showbiz hat.

Nevin For Everton

When we were struggling, you could give Pat Nevin the ball and he'd always take it forward with this carefree approach to the game. Even if he was going to lose it, he'd always take men on. This sounds terrible but I even went to see Nevin play for Everton when they came to Arsenal. They stuck him out on the wing and never gave him the ball. Shows how much I liked him. He was a completely unselfish player. He wouldn't take men on just for the sake of it, but when he did he was brilliant. He was the type of player who'd slow down to allow the opposition to catch up with him, just so that he could beat them again.

Nigel Falconer

All-Time Great

Pat Nevin was absolutely charming. He was more interested in talking about the arts and living in London than about football. Of course, he was a tremendous player too. If Nevin had played in the 1930s or '40s, he would be mentioned in the Tom Finney and Stanley Matthews category.

Scott Cheshire

Heroic Stalwarts Of Defence

Although finishing only ninth in the league in the 1921-22 campaign, the battling strengths of Meehan and Smith meant that Chelsea's defensive record was bettered only by champions, Liverpool, and runners-up, Tottenham Hotspur.

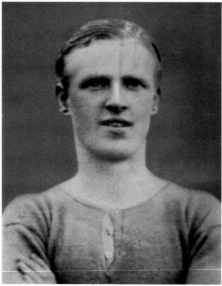

Tommy Meehan.

George Smith.

It's Elliott!

I was in a pub recently when my friend went, 'It's Elliott! It's Elliott!' I turned round and Paul Elliott was standing just a couple of paces away from me. I've always admired him but didn't have the courage to go up and say anything. I mean, what do you say? Hello, I support Chelsea? I watched you play and I think you're really great? I'd feel really silly. He looked in superb shape still. It was such a shame that his career ended so early.

Linda Richmond

A Lovely Geezer

Last year, me and the missus were shopping in Marks & Spencers when we spotted Paul Elliott. She said, 'I've got to get his autograph!' Well, the only paper I had on me, for writing on, was the ticket stub from the Bruges' Cup Winners' Cup game. So she went over with it and he signed it. Lovely geezer as it turned out! He even asked my wife's advice on baby clothes!

Nick Davis

Glenn Hoddle's last game as manager of Chelsea Football Club, against Blackburn Rovers on 5th May 1996.

Glenn Hoddle

Glenn Hoddle was a great player and was showing all the signs of becoming a great manager for us. I was really upset when he left Stamford Bridge to manage the national team. Fortunately, Ruud Gullit took hold of the reins and continued Hoddle's good work.

Nick Hines

The Best Player Ever

If I could be any Chelsea player, I would be Gullit. I adored him even before he came to Chelsea. This was a man who dedicated his European Footballer Of The Year Award to Nelson Mandela. At the time, some people wouldn't even have known who Mandela was. Gullit's just got everything: he's funny, he's articulate, he's a guy I can imagine going for a drink with. Never mind how much I love Chelsea, there aren't many players I can imagine doing that with. Gullit, to me, is the best player we've had ever. I was devastated when he left the club.

Ron Coello

Lemonade Bottles

Ruud Gullit was a great manager. That man had a vision. Who else, when 2-0 down at half-time to Liverpool in the cup, could explain to the players how to win that game? He made one substitution and changed the tactics around. Apparently at Spurs once, when we scored five in the second half, he used lemonade bottles to illustrate positional play to the players at half-time. Brilliant!

Peter Scherschel

Big Nose!

I'll never forget Ruud Gullit joining the club – one of the few real world-class players we've had. He was probably Glenn Hoddle's best signing for us. He arrived at Stamford Bridge and Dennis Wise called him 'big nose'! I imagine Dennis is one of the blokes who says, 'Okay, you may be getting paid £10,000 a week more than us but you're at Stamford Bridge now and you're one of the boys! You dig in and we all play together!' Dennis creates a great team spirit – he's a great captain. He's been at Chelsea for ten years and for me, he is the club.

Tim Lovejoy

Mascot Peter Coello warms up with the players for Hoddle's last game in charge.

Mascot Peter Coello meets Chelsea's 'best ever player'.

The Nicest Bloke

When people talk about Dennis Wise being hard it makes me laugh, because he's just the nicest bloke you could hope to meet.

Andy Jacobs

Dennis Wise - True blue.

Famous Last Words

I met 'Wisie' four or five years ago, in a pub after the boat race. I spent about half an hour talking to him about Chelsea. He was really nice – well friendly. It was just before the team were due to fly out to Zaragoza in the Cup Winners' Cup. Dennis told me that they were going to go out there and play for the draw. We lost the game 3-0. Famous last words!

Jamie Roberts

Blue Blood

I come from the north of England and I only started supporting Chelsea a few years ago, when I moved down south. I still support my home town team, so I consider Chelsea my second club. This gives me a bit of a different perspective to most Chelsea fans. Having been on the other side of the fence, let me tell you that amongst away supporters, Dennis Wise is not the most popular of players. I'm trying hard to be diplomatic here, but let's just say that they see him as a bit of a hard man with a suspect attitude. Which is ridiculous, because if you go see him week in week out, you soon learn that his attitude is exemplary. Cut Dennis Wise open and he bleeds blue and white, I'm sure. And his reading of the game and his passing are second to none. In fact, it's a national disgrace that he's overlooked for England these days. I guess, if I'm really honest, I'd have to say that the reason away fans love to hate Dennis, is that they'd give anything to have a player with his commitment playing in their team.

Nick Hines

Heart On His Sleeve

Dennis Wise wears his heart on his sleeve. When he's enjoying himself, you can feel it.

Nigel Falconer

Call Me Dennis

I read somewhere that Dennis Bergkamp's parents named him after Dennis Law. I think that in the future, all children in the West London area called Dennis or Denise will have been named in honour of 'Wisie', Chelsea's own patron saint of skill.

Nick Hines

La-la-la-Zola!

Zola is my favourite player because of his skills. When he's under pressure, he always manages to keep possession. When my boyfriend arrived back from the Cup Winners' Cup Final in Stockholm, he rang me up from the airport. I'd watched the game on TV and had seen Zola score the winner. I couldn't stop myself from singing down the line, 'La-la-la Zola! La-la-la-Zola!'

I'm going to try and book a room in the Chelsea hotel for my boyfriend's birthday. I don't really know what to expect, but if I get a choice of duvet cover, I'll ask for the Zola one, obviously!

Sue Hawkins

Fans celebrate Zola's winning goal in Stockholm, 1998.

SECTION FOUR

CHAMPIONSHIP CHEERS AND CUP FINAL TEARS

Success, as supporters of Chelsea are aware, is a strange beast. Just when you think it's within touching distance, you turn your back for a moment and it shoots off into the distance. And when you eventually catch up with it, and begin to harbour thoughts of nurturing it and allowing it to grow, it escapes and goes on the run for twenty-odd years! Here, from the championship-winning triumph of 1955, in front of Stamford Bridge's home fans, through to the heartbreaking FA Cup defeat of 1994, Chelsea fans share with us their encounters and near experiences with the animal known as success.

Wembley, 1994.

The team are presented with the championship trophy in 1955.

Champions!

When Chelsea won the championship in 1955, it was absolutely fantastic. But what a lot of people don't realise about that season is that we didn't take over the leadership until the last week of March, when we won away to Cardiff. That was when people really started to get excited. There was a newspaper strike at the time and the only 'paper you could get in London was the *Manchester Guardian*. So most people listened to the radio to find out how Chelsea were doing.

We had a great team back then. One of the linchpins was John Harris, who'd just moved from centre-half to full-back. Ron Greenwood, who had joined us as a boy at the end of the 1930s, played the first half of that season, and he and Stan Wicks were the great pillars of defence. Behind them, either Bill Robertson or Chic Thomson kept goal.

Ken Armstrong and Derek Saunders were the wing-halves and were as different as two players could be: Armstrong was a calm constructive player, whereas Saunders was tough and hard tackling.

Roy Bentley in the forward line was magnificent – one of the finest headers of the ball I ever saw. Alongside him was John McNichol, who was a typical Scottish ball player.

Finally, Eric Parsons, or 'The Rabbit' as he was known, and Jim Lewis, were our wingers. Lewis would poach a lot of goals for us.

Scott Cheshire

Ken Armstrong – Calm and constructive.

The Championship Comes To Chelsea At Last

It was a red letter day at Stamford Bridge on Saturday. The two solid points that the 3-0 victory over Sheffield Wednesday brought to Chelsea made 23rd April 1955 a date that will always be remembered down West London way. In years to come men will tell their grandchildren that this was the afternoon they saw Chelsea gain their first major prize in football by becoming champions of the Football League.

The Times,
Monday 25th April 1955

The Rabbit

We had a great team in the '50s. 'Bunny' Parsons on the wing was fantastic. And the 'keeper, Bill Robertson, was very keen. I remember one game where Chelsea were losing by three or four goals and he rushed out to take a free-kick with five minutes to go. People were shouting out for him not to bother.

Stan Falconer

Bill Robertson – Very keen!

On the ground, looking through the net, Eric Parsons – 'The Rabbit'. This was Chelsea's first goal in the 3-0 win over Sheffield Wednesday that clinched the championship.

Speeches All Round

We won the championship in front of our fans, at home to Sheffield Wednesday. We won 3-0, which was made easier by the fact that the Wednesday goalkeeper was carried off early on. Of course, there were no substitutes in those days.

There were marvellous celebrations after the final whistle. All the players came out and sat in front of the old Directors' Box in the East Stand. Joe Mears, the chairman, made a speech. Then Ted Drake, the manager, made a speech, then John Harris, then Roy Bentley. We didn't get away until nearly six o'clock.

Of course, looking back, it was just as well that we enjoyed the occasion to the full. It would be ten long years before another domestic success came our way, with the League Cup triumph of 1965. After that, we only had to wait another two years for a real crack at one of the big trophies – the FA Cup.

Scott Cheshire

Roy Bentley – Captain of the championship-winning team of 1955.

Bentley scoring against Spurs at Stamford Bridge.

Spurs Triumph In The 1967 'Cockney Cup Final'

Chelsea Football Club failed to prove themselves in the cockney derby, as Tottenham took the honours with a 2-1 win in the FA Cup Final on Saturday. Chelsea captain Ron Harris, aged only 22, would have been the youngest player to take the cup from the Royal Box, had Chelsea triumphed. As it was, he at least set his side an example of indomitable spirit. Chelsea, as a whole, won the plaudits as good losers of a sporting match.

The Times, Monday 22nd May 1967

Wembley Defeat

I went to the 1967 FA Cup Final, when we lost to Tottenham. They allocated tickets on a voucher basis back then – there would be a voucher on the back of every programme for you to collect. You had to gather together a certain number of vouchers before you could apply for a Wembley ticket. I only started going in January but up to then, Chelsea hadn't had a lot of success. So one way or another, I managed to cobble together sixteen of these vouchers. It was a case of me having to beg, steal or borrow them, and I eventually had enough for a Cup Final ticket. I was fifteen at the time. I went to Wembley with some relatives. We all had seats in different blocks and I had to sit all by myself. I managed to persuade the guy manning the turnstile to let me in with the others, so that we could all watch the match together. Tottenham beat us 2-1 and I cried my eyes out.

Linda Richmond

The Elusive Ticket

I couldn't get a ticket for the 1967 FA Cup Final. That season I'd been to virtually all the home games and bought programmes. I'd discarded them, only to discover that there were vouchers on the back that would be useful later. When it was announced that you could use the vouchers to get a Wembley ticket, I desperately tried to get hold of all the programmes, but it was too late.

Andy Jackson

Right: Peter Bonetti – Chelsea's 'keeper in the 1967 FA Cup Final.

The Missing Voucher

I had a full set of vouchers for Wembley in 1967. I posted them to the club and they wrote back saying that one was missing. They said that I couldn't have a ticket. I was so gutted that I took my Aunt Doris over to Chelsea with me and she warned them, 'I'm not moving from this ticket office until you give this boy his ticket!' We stood there for half an hour, until eventually they caved in and they gave me a Cup Final ticket. Having gone through all that, it was a terrible game.

Kevin Ryan

Terry Venables – Although pictured here in his Chelsea days, he would contribute to the Blues downfall in the 1967 'Cockney Cup Final'.

Tambling Salvages Some Pride

Wembley 1967 was a real let-down because we just didn't play. Tottenham had signed Terry Venables and won easily. Bobby Tambling got a late goal for us, which gave the score-sheet a false impression.

Scott Cheshire

Sick As A Dog

In the 1960s, there used to be dog races at Stamford Bridge every Thursday afternoon and Saturday night, even when Chelsea played at home. On the night of the '67 Cup Final I was down at The Bridge for the dogs, when the team arrived back on the bus. There were no celebrations, no nothing – the players just got in their cars and drove away. They didn't even hang around to watch the dogs.

Stan Falconer

Chelsea Seize Cup In Epic Final Replay

The treadmill is over – a new name is on the FA Cup. One of the most punishing finals in modern history – perhaps all history – began at Wembley with extra-time over a fortnight ago, and ended last night at Old Trafford, Manchester, again in extra-time. Looking back over the long struggles of that 2-2 drawn first encounter and yesterday's 2-1 replay victory, we can now say that Chelsea came three times from behind to match the league champions of last year and finally snatched the winner fourteen minutes into the extra-time period.

So, with an historic touch, Chelsea have finally won the prize which they first played for at Old Trafford in the final of 1915, when Sheffield United beat them.

Geoffrey Green, *The Times*, Thursday 30th April 1970

Television Coverage

I remember the Cup Finals of '67 and '70. I watched them on TV, because I couldn't get a ticket. Our TV was still black and white. Colour televisions were around at the time, but only the well-off people could afford them.

Jim McSweeney

Boys And Football

I didn't go to the 1970 Cup Final nor the replay. I watched them on television and it just wasn't the same as being there. That year and the following year were actually the two seasons I saw the least games. I was thinking about getting married and boys were more important than football – but only very, very briefly!

Linda Richmond

David Webb – Fantastic in the '70s, not half-bad two decades later! Seen here playing a charity game in the '90s.

Glory At Old Trafford

The 1970 FA Cup Final was absolutely tremendous, because, before the late equaliser at Wembley, everyone had given up. Leeds looked the better side and Eddie Gray was giving David Webb a terrible run around. For long periods we were really outplayed.

I went to Old Trafford for the replay. David Webb moved into the middle and Ron Harris moved to full back. It was one of the most dramatic nights of football I can remember. Peter Bonetti went down injured. Harry Medhurst was the trainer then and I can see him now down at the Stretford End, tending to Bonetti, for what seemed like an age. Eventually he limped to his feet. With no substitutes, Dave Webb would have had to go in goal for us.

The two goals were great. I remember that marvellous through ball from Charlie Cooke, headed into the net by Osgood. The winning goal was magnificent. Hutchinson took a long throw, the ball brushed Jackie Charlton's head, and Webb climbed and put it in the net.

I went to Stamford Bridge when the trophy was brought back. Fulham Road was a sea of blue and white and this open-top bus, carrying the players, came inching along to the old town hall. There was absolute delirium.

Scott Cheshire

Harry Medhurst – The great 'keeper of the '50s, who would later assume training responsibilities at Stamford Bridge.

Terrace Ticket Number 2

The 1970 Cup Final was the first to be replayed for over fifty years. Chelsea had used the voucher system to sell their tickets for the first game and didn't know how to allocate tickets fairly for the replay. I wrote to the club with a couple of ideas and in return, they gave me a ticket for the replay free of charge. It was terrace ticket Number 2, Stretford End, and it had 'J.B. Mears' written on the back. I think it came from the old chairman's son.

I carry that ticket around with me everywhere, now. I've shown it to many people over the years.

I took my thirteen-year-old sister to that game. She hadn't been to a game before and, to the best of my knowledge, she's never been to a game since.

Kevin Ryan

The League Cup

The first time I went to Wembley was for the 1972 League Cup Final against Stoke, which we lost 2-1. It was a good day out, but I was extremely disappointed at the result. Particularly because defeat had never entered my head before the game. When Osgood equalised before half-time, it seemed a forgone conclusion that we would go on to win. I didn't stay to see the presentation afterwards, I just went home. It's said that you should stay to cheer your team on afterwards, but I was just too disappointed.

I went to the FA Cup Final in 1994 too, when we lost to Manchester United. A friend of mine was a family season ticket holder and thought that his boy of seven was too young to go – so he took me instead. Another friend of mine managed to get a ticket on the black market for £250, and had to sit in the Man United end. That day was another marvellous occasion spoilt by the game.

Paul Fisher

Bukta *professional sportwear*

Peter Osgood thinks it's the greatest!

Star forward for Cup-Winners Chelsea and the England World Cup Team, Peter Osgood certainly knows a thing or two about football kits! And he says: 'If you're going all out to play well, you've got to have well-designed kit—and for a really professional look you just can't beat Bukta Sportwear. They're winners for hard wear, too'.

Ask your **local sports outfitter** for the FREE Bukta 1970 World Cup Catalogue, packed with kits in all the top soccer and rugby club colours—over 1,000 different colour combinations of jerseys, shirts, shorts and stockings!

OR write for a copy to: Edward R. Buck & Sons Ltd., Bukta House, Brinksway, Stockport, Cheshire.

JULY, 1970   17

Peter Osgood – Striker without equal.

Sitting With The Enemy

We got hold of tickets for the 1972 League Cup Final via the black market. We were stuck in with the Stoke supporters, which was awful. Not only did we see Chelsea lose, but we had to watch the people around us celebrating.

I also went to the Full Members Cup in 1986 against Manchester City. We only just won 5-4, after having led 5-1 at one stage. Everybody made fun of us before the final, saying that it was a 'Mickey Mouse competition'. I didn't care though. It was still important to me because Chelsea were going to be at Wembley – and no one could argue with that. And the match turned out to be so exciting. To think, we were walking away with the game and then nearly managed to blow it. I was so nervous by the end of it that I couldn't stop biting my fingernails.

Linda Richmond

Mickey Mouse Cup

That Full Members Cup Final was some match. We were 5-1 up with a few minutes go and City scored a few quick goals. The crowds were treated to a goal-feast! Because it was a 'Mickey Mouse cup', nobody expected the crowd to be so big. There were 68,000 people there and 50,000 of those were supporting Chelsea. It was in the days when Wembley held 100,000 and we managed to sell our whole allocation of tickets.

I next went to Wembley for the Zenith Data Systems Cup, in 1990, when we played Middlesborough. We won 1-0. The week before the final, we played Arsenal in the league. Johnny Bumstead scored for us. It was the first time we'd beaten Arsenal in ages. The Arsenal fans were making fun of us – the usual stuff about us going to Wembley for a pointless competition. But we didn't care – we were excited about Wembley and we'd just beaten them 1-0. The game at Wembley the following week was terrible.

Kevin Wilson – One of the starting eleven in Chelsea's ranks for the ZDS Cup Final appearance in 1990.

Nick Davis

A Dreadful Game

The Zenith Data game against Middlesborough was awful, even though we won. I go to most England games and so I've seen a lot of dreadful games at Wembley. That final against Boro ranks as one of the worst I've ever seen.

Barry Jones

Chelsea celebrate their ZDS Cup victory, 1990.

FA Cup Heartbreak As Manchester United Put Four Past Chelsea

Down in the Wembley tunnel on Saturday, away from the neon scoreboard that flashed up the deserved if exaggerated 4-0 result, dejection mingled with elation. Chelsea's beaten, competitive captain, Dennis Wise, the picture of this dejection, had been beyond consolation. Glenn Hoddle, the Chelsea player-manager, had indeed been justified to claim: 'For sixty minutes, we did more than hold them. We were the better team when the game was tight and we were under pressure. It's bad enough losing the Cup Final – but we didn't deserve that score.'

Rob Hughes, *The Times*, Monday 16th May 1994

The Hen Party

I went through every avenue I could to get a ticket for the Cup Final in 1994. I ended up getting two from the Metropolitan Police Athletics Association, of all places.

After all my efforts to get tickets, the whole day was appalling. I'd agreed with my brother that we'd walk to Sudbury Town Tube Station after the game. I'd read in some magazine that that was the best way to get home from Wembley – that there wouldn't be as many crowds as at nearer stations. So we set off walking and it started to rain. We walked for what seemed liked ages and got soaked. It became apparent that the tube station was too far away to walk to, so we caught a bus. We were very cold and wet by this time.

We went to a pub in Sloane Square and I don't really remember much about the evening. We got very very drunk, which seemed the only thing to do after losing 4-0 in the Cup Final. There was a hen-party in the pub that night. The bride-to-be was wearing a wedding-veil and had an L-plate tied to her back. I don't know what her and her friends must have thought about us – all these Chelsea fans raising the roof singing rude songs about Man United.

Richard Sharp

Wembley Stadium is turned blue for the FA Cup Final of 1994, against Manchester United.

A Match To Forget

The first final I went to was the Full Members Cup in 1986 when we beat Manchester City. Winning at Wembley felt really cool, although it didn't feel like a real cup. When I went to the FA Cup Final in 1994 it felt like I was at a proper final. We lost 4-0 to Manchester United and I find it hard to talk about that defeat. Beforehand, I was really sure that we were going to win. The disappointment was so great that I've now managed to erase that game from my memory. Someone was talking to me recently about United's goals and I had to say, 'Look, I can just about remember the score!' It was incredibly depressing, having waited so long for Chelsea to do something. I left Wembley feeling really down and just went straight home. I really don't talk about that game anymore.

Tim Lovejoy

So Bad It Hurts

For the final in 1994 my son really went to town. He painted his face blue, wore his scarf and even wrapped himself in a blue Batman cape. Unfortunately, on the way into the ground, he slipped on the Wembley steps and cracked his face. He cut his lip and his eye and was really badly shaken. Obviously my first concern was for my son. My second concern was for the game – we'd waited twenty-odd years to get to the Cup Final and we were probably going to be spending it in casualty. I managed to clean him up a bit and we decided to watch the game anyway. So we struggled to our seats, sat through the whole thing and watched Chelsea lose 4-0. Next to us was a bloke with four kids and after the first goal went in, one of the kids started crying. He was about seven-years-old and didn't stop sobbing for the rest of the game.

Nigel Falconer

Silver Paper Cup

There was a little boy next to me who'd made a little cup out of silver paper. At the end of the match he ripped it up and started crying. That started me off sobbing. It's got to go down as the worst day of my whole life.

Jacquie Clarke

'I've made my own cup!' – Fans leave Wembley after the shattering 4-0 defeat.

An Empty Office

I couldn't get a ticket for Wembley in '94. I had to go to work anyway, so I got into the office and set up a television to watch the match. The place was empty. I was glad that nobody else was around because I literally cried at the end. I went straight down the pub afterwards. All my friends who had gone to Wembley started to arrive with their flags, looking miserable and forlorn.

Daryl Woodward

We did our best – The team returns to Fulham Broadway in 1994, without the cup.

My Favourite Band

Even though Chelsea lost, the whole day and the atmosphere were still mind-blowing. It was like going to a performance of your all-time favourite band that you've waited decades to see.

Jan Bettis

A Miserable Holiday

The FA Cup semi-final in 1994, against Luton, was played at Wembley. I couldn't go because my mum had booked us a holiday to Tunisia months previously without thinking about the fixture list. We were struggling against relegation for a long time that season and I'd been to all the games. I couldn't believe my bad luck when we got to the semi-final and I couldn't make it. I was desperate to see the game. I would much rather have gone to the match than Tunisia. But I had no choice in the matter. My mum tried to console me by saying that I could always watch the game via satellite television on holiday.

As it happened, our hotel was the only place with satellite television in the resort. Days before the match, I asked the bloke in charge of the TV if I could watch the game. He said that it would be okay. On the day of the game, I went into the television lounge to take my seat. There were loads of kids watching *The A Team* on another channel. The bloke in charge said that he wouldn't change the channel until the programme had finished.

The A Team seemed to last forever. It was dubbed in German, so I couldn't even follow the story. I have hated Mr T ever since, although I used to really like him when I was little. Eventually it finished and it was then I discovered that the satellite dish could not pick up the channel showing the game anyway. I was really upset that I couldn't see Chelsea.

Worse was to follow. The telephones wouldn't work in the hotel after the match had finished. I couldn't phone my dad to find out the result. I had to wait until the next day when we were travelling home, before I could find out the score. A man in our queue at the Tunisian airport told me Chelsea had won. I was still a bit worried that it might not be true and only relaxed when I saw it in a newspaper at Gatwick Airport. We had beaten Luton 2-0.

If this happened again, there is no way I would go on holiday. Not knowing the result until the next day was torture. I was so miserable on holiday that I think my mum now understands that I am not joking when I say, 'Football is my life.'

Ross Falconer

GOODBYE, MATTHEW

Matthew Harding, a Director of Chelsea Football Club and a lifelong fan, was killed in a tragic helicopter crash on 23rd October 1996. The pilot and four others onboard also lost their lives. They had been returning from a League Cup fixture at Bolton Wanderers.

Matthew Harding's death both shocked and deeply saddened the world of football. In the days following the tragedy, supporters flocked to Stamford Bridge, leaving behind scarves and other club memorabilia at the gates, as a mark of their respect. The next game, at home to Tottenham Hotspur, was an emotional experience for all. During a minute's silence before kick-off, the players held hands around the centre-spot, where a pint of Guinness, Matthew's favourite tipple, had been placed. Matthew Harding was already a hero to many fans, who saw him as a supporter first and foremost, who just happened to have the means and drive to rise to the club's board of control. When he died, Chelsea fans lost one of their own.

Fans send a special message to the players, on the eve of Chelsea's European Cup Winners' Cup Final appearance, 1998.

The News Breaks

I woke up in the morning and the news had broken. I had to go into work at Sky Television but I was in a daze. I just sat there all day, with people coming up to me and asking if I had a contact number for this Chelsea player or that Chelsea player. Although Sky handled the news really well, they obviously had to look at it in a different way to how I was looking at it. I was in a real depression. I never got to meet Matthew, but we'd spoken to the club about him coming on our Saturday morning show. I think that would have been great. Being a well-known Chelsea fan on television, I got an unbelievable number of letters from people who didn't know who else to write to. There was a huge post-bag from fans saying how sorry they were about the whole thing. We had to put together a show for the weekend and I just didn't know what to do. It was a really tough time to be a fan. I went to the Tottenham game after it happened. The atmosphere was confusing with so many people dazed. Football is football because of the fans and on that day, the fans were dazed and the whole thing was subdued. People didn't really know how to react.

Tim Lovejoy

A Pint Of Guinness

I heard about Harding's accident on the morning radio. I couldn't believe it. I only saw the guy once, at the '96 semi-final against Manchester United at Villa Park. We lost 2-1 and Harding and chairman Ken Bates were right behind us. When Gullit scored for us, I saw Matthew Harding jumping all over the place. I'll never forget the first game after the accident, when we beat Tottenham 3-1. A wreath was laid on the centre-circle and a pint of Guinness was put next to it. My friend's nephew was mascot for the day and joined hands with the players during the minute's silence. It was quite a day for him – certainly one to tell the grandchildren.

Richard Sharp

The captains line up before the Tottenham match – Note the wreath and pint of Guinness to the right of the picture.

The Saddest Game

The Tottenham match was the most emotional game I'd ever been to. It was really sad and when the players came on with the wreath I just couldn't help crying. To see the players holding hands around the centre-circle was something I've never seen before, nor want to see again. The tears were just running down my face. The Tottenham fans were exemplary. They were brilliant that day.

Linda Richmond

Rivalry And Respect

I dislike Tottenham but my whole opinion of them changed that day. They showed great respect and conducted themselves superbly. That's the way football should be: rivalry, but with a show of respect.

Andy Jackson

Scarf On The Pitch

When we went down to Chelsea for the Tottenham match, there were people walking around bare-chested because they'd thrown down their shirts at the gates. I was really really moved by it all. I had a tear in my eye that day and my son threw his scarf on the pitch.

Nigel Falconer

A Moving Time

The atmosphere was very eerie. The silence before the game was spooky – you couldn't even hear the traffic. I've never experienced anything like that before. It was very moving.

Paul Fisher

Blue And White Army

The first away game after Harding's accident was at Old Trafford, where we beat them 2-1. The Chelsea fans were just a wall of noise that day. The first thing the Man United fans sang was, 'Where's your famous Munich song?' – a reference to the chant about the Munich air disaster that away supporters sometimes sing in bad taste. The Chelsea fans retorted, 'Matthew Harding's blue and white army.' And the Manchester fans stood up and applauded us. It was really moving.

Ron Coello

A young supporter stands on the hallowed turf; in the background, building work continues on the new North Stand. When completed, the stand was named 'The Matthew Harding North Stand', in honour of Matthew's memory.

The Chelsea Messiah

I met Matthew Harding a couple of times on trains to away games. He often travelled with his two kids. He was very approachable. He was a big big fan. I like to think, however, that if I had as much money as Harding, I'd invest just as much in the club – I'd be the new Chelsea messiah.

Barry Jones

Win It For Matthew

We had a banner made for the Cup Winners' Cup Final in Stockholm that read, 'Win it for Matthew'. We decided that, come what may, we'd burn it after the game.

Jacquie Clarke

A Casual Conversation

I once met Matthew Harding at a Chelsea dinner-dance in 1994 or '95. It was around Christmas time and I'd taken my camera along. This rather flamboyant woman came up and said, 'Would you take a picture of me and Matthew?' I said, 'I don't know, you'd better ask his permission.' She didn't return so I thought no more about it. After about an hour, I saw Matthew at the bar on his own. I asked if the woman had got her wish and had her picture taken with him. He replied, 'Yes – I was just glad to get away from her. She'd been after me all night!' And then we got into this casual conversation, like you would with any guy in a pub.

I met him again the following season, when my nephew, Peter, was mascot for Glenn Hoddle's last game in charge. He was a lovely guy. I talked to him for twenty minutes about this and that.

When my mum rang me at work and told me that Harding had died, I didn't know what to say. My family had been looking forward to the next game, against Tottenham, because my other nephew, Bobby, had been chosen to be mascot. So the whole week leading up to that game seemed really strange.

On the day of the game, my nephew came out with the players and started to warm up. Dennis Wise went up to him, put his arm around his shoulders and quietly told him that the players wouldn't be warming up this time – that it was a bit different. My nephew got to hold hands with the players and was on *Match Of The Day*. It was all a very odd occasion. The Tottenham fans were really good that day. Really quiet and respectful.

Ron Coello

Peter and Bobby Coello meet Tony Banks MP, before the Tottenham match.

PINCH ME,
I MUST BE DREAMING

Shame on those who say that dreams only come true in fairy tales. For after a major trophy-winning drought of twenty-six years, Chelsea finally did the unthinkable and triumphed on Wembley's hallowed turf in the FA Cup Final of 1997. It was Chelsea's first real success since Dave Sexton's boys had won the FA Cup and then gone on to European glory, in the '70s. Over two decades of lost chances and broken promises were finally washed away, as opponents Middlesbrough were swept aside in a thrilling finale to the season. And after such a long wait, all it took, in the end, were forty-three seconds on the clock and a certain Italian.

Fans, Paul King (left) and Jason Samut get 'a little excited' over Chelsea's FA Cup success, 1997.

Di Matteo's Lightening Strike Paves The Way

Roberto Di Matteo produced the fastest goal in an FA Cup final at Wembley on Saturday, after just 43 seconds. His spectacular strike, a big dipper, eclipsed Jackie Milburn's 45-second curtain-raiser for Newcastle United in 1955. Striking the ball on the run from nearly 30 yards, he caught Ben Roberts in the opposing goal just far enough off his line for the ball to beat him overhead before dipping late, under the bar. A marvellous goal to behold, it was a terrible one to concede.

As early as that first minute, it left opponents Middlesbrough looking deflated and demoralised – a defeat waiting to happen. Any lingering doubt of a Chelsea victory was removed eight minutes from the end, when Eddie Newton stabbed the ball past Roberts from five yards, giving the Blues a 2-0 win.

Joe Lovejoy, The Sunday Times, 18th May 1997

My Blue Jester's Hat!

The FA Cup Final in 1997 was absolutely fantastic. It was the best day of my entire life – absolutely wonderful. I left home at half past eight in the morning and didn't get back until eight at night. My friends had booked a restaurant for the evening and I went along all dressed up with my face still painted and still wearing my blue jester's hat. I was really nervous before the game but we only had to wait a short space of time for Chelsea to score. That must have really demoralised Middlesbrough. Their fans were really friendly before and after the game. I felt a bit sorry for them.

Linda Richmond

Three Generations Together

I took my son, my dad and my girlfriend. It was a really emotional day, having three generations together. You can't buy something like that. My dad was quite overawed by the intensity of it all. He's pretty arthritic, an old retired carpet-fitter – but I must admit that when Di Matteo scored after forty-three seconds, my dad was out of his seat punching the air. When you bear in mind the fact that he weighs twenty-two stone, you can imagine that it's quite a sight.

Nigel Falconer

The players warm up before their appointment with destiny, Wembley, 1997.

Just Like Kids

When Di Matteo scored I went absolutely mad. My dad was with me and he's sixty-five, but we just jumped around like little kids. When you're 1-0 up after only forty-three seconds you can relax and enjoy the game. Especially when you know that the team you're playing is worse than you by a long way. The semi-final that year against Luton was good too. Kerry Dixon got a good reception. He was a great favourite of the Chelsea fans.

Barry Jones

The pre-match ceremony, Wembley, 1997.

Street Parties

When Di Matteo scored I didn't think it had gone in. Then I thought, 'It's a goal!' Seconds later I was on the floor, with everyone on top of me! The rest of the game went really slowly. We had to wait with baited-breath for Eddie Newton to score right at the end.

Afterwards, it felt vaguely surreal – we couldn't believe we'd won. We went back to Marylebone and hit a few pubs around there. We then went back to Fulham Road to be near Stamford Bridge. There were street–parties going on down there. A lot of pubs were selling cans over the counter and people were drinking outside. I got very very drunk that night. I wasn't too well the next day. I had to take my wife out for a meal, to apologise for turning up in such a state the night before.

Stop the clock! – Roberta Di Matteo, 'the 43-second man' in pre-Wembley training session.

Richard Sharp

The Cup Comes Home

I completely and utterly expected us to win the cup. There was this buzz about us and I was just sure that we'd win. It was a really exciting time. I was in the pubs with the fans beforehand and having a sing-song. It was great – just the way football should be.

Di Matteo scoring in the first minute

We've done it! – The players collect their winners' medals – and a pat on the back from chairman Ken Bates.

took all the pressure off us and I thoroughly enjoyed the game. It was maybe not the most classic cup final of all-time, but I didn't care. All the way home I was talking to other fans and singing songs on the train. It was one of the best days of my life.

Tim Lovejoy

Great Celebration

The players had a tremendous celebration after the game. It was probably the longest any team has ever stayed on the pitch after a final. After the game, I went straight down the King's Road, just as I had after we'd won the Cup Winners' Cup twenty-six years before. It was just one big party down there.

Andy Jackson

Solid gold! – Kevin Hitchcock shows off his gong.

Sleepless Night

For me the final was horrible from start to finish, because I was terrified we'd throw it away. I really enjoyed all the games in the run-up, but not the final. I just wanted it to be over and done with, because I'd waited so long for this moment of pleasure. Not even Di Matteo scoring so early on relaxed me. I've always said that Chelsea are at their most dangerous when they're 1-0 up. So until Newton got the second, and I knew we were going to do it, I couldn't enjoy the game. I was just too tense. The night before I couldn't sleep.

After the game it was superb. I really enjoyed myself and started to think about what I'd say to colleagues at work. I've got this thing that when we lose on a Saturday, I have to try and imagine what people at work will say to me on Monday morning, so that I can defend myself. But I'd never prepared, in my mind, what I'd say if we won something. I never expected that to happen.

Ron Coello

Street parties – Fans celebrate the Wembley success.

Idle Threat

The misery of the 1994 defeat made it all the better when we did eventually win. I always said that when Chelsea won something, I'd stop going. It was an idle threat of course because I never expected us to win anything.

Nigel Falconer

Chelsea Underpants

I didn't want to take my wife to Wembley in '97. I'd taken her in 1994, when we'd lost, so I'd assumed that she was unlucky. I decided to give her a second chance and she really enjoyed it. To actually win something was very special. I'd promised the kids that if

All smiles – Chelsea fan Rob Sheldon in happy mood after the final whistle.

Chelsea ever won something I'd dance in my underpants in the street singing 'Chelsea! Chelsea!' And I did it! One of the neighbours came storming out of his house wondering what was going on.

Andy Jacobs

A Major Trophy At Last

Had we not beaten Middlesbrough, it would have been a bitter blow. I went with four others, but I was the only one who'd seen us win a major trophy. We were all really thrilled but I don't think my excitement quite matched theirs. One of the other chaps was in tears. I think the difference between 1997 and 1970 was that against Middlesbrough we expected to win, whereas against Leeds we only hoped to win.

Scott Cheshire

Tickled blue! – Two young ladies leave no doubt as to who they support, Wembley, 1997.

The Longest Night

The club decided to sell Cup Final tickets to members all through the night, starting at eight o'clock in the evening. The idea was just to carry on selling until all the tickets were gone. So I took a half-day off work and got there at about quarter past four.

There were thousands already in the queue. It went from the main

The Clarke family in pre-match cup presentation.

entrance, right past the East Stand and around to the North Stand. I queued for eight hours and eventually got my hands on a ticket at half past midnight. The time went quite quickly. A few of us had a whip round in the night and somebody went off to get a few cans of beer. Later on, we had another whip round and someone was despatched to get a bottle of whisky. So we stood in the queue and had a few scotches!

When I finally got my ticket and left through the front gate, there were people offering me a couple of hundred pounds for it. If I'd queued up for half and hour I might have been tempted to sell it, but not after eight hours.

Paul Fisher

Money Well Spent

I entered the club scheme where you bought shares in the pitch. It you did this then you were assured of Wembley tickets. I suppose you could say that I ended up paying about £460 for two tickets, but it was worth every single penny.

Jamie Roberts

Fans wait at Fulham Broadway for a glimpse of the team bringing the cup home to Stamford Bridge.

Trafalgar Square

I went to Wembley in 1997 with a cousin of mine who I had hardly seen in twenty years. He plays for an amateur football club and got a couple of Cup Final tickets through them. Afterwards, we went to the West End to celebrate and ended up going night-clubbing. The idea was for him to stay at my place after the final since it was quite a distance for him to travel home. By the time we'd finished partying, it was so late that he thought he'd stay in London and wait for the dawn to arrive. Then he could travel home straight from the capital. He ended up sleeping on a bench in Trafalgar Square.

Daryl Woodward

Here they come – The team bus inches along towards Stamford Bridge.

The cup is held aloft for all the Blue Army to see.

Chelsea International

The day before the game, I went to a pre-Cup Final party at the Sporting Rat pub on Fulham Road. It had been organised by the members of a Chelsea Internet mailing list. I turned up and there were about a hundred people there. We had a quarter of the pub cordoned off for ourselves. Out of those hundred people, only ten were from the UK. There were twenty South Africans, a bloke from Singapore and a couple of Malaysians. There were a few Australians and even an guy who had flown in from Toronto for the final. I was the token German. The only thing we had in common was that we all supported Chelsea. I'd hoped that with a little bit of luck I might be able to pick up a ticket for the final. Maybe someone from abroad had missed their flight? An English guy thought he could lay his hands on a spare ticket and told me to wait by my phone on the morning of the game. I was praying that the telephone would ring – but it never did. So I didn't get to see us lift the trophy at Wembley. Of course I've been to Wembley since, on the very happy occasion of seeing Germany beat England. Some people think it strange that I support an English league team, but the German national side.

Peter Scherschel

What the 'papers said – A montage of newspaper headlines, heralding Chelsea's FA Cup success.

A Real 'Pea Souper'

I went to all the cup matches leading up to Wembley. I remember going to Portsmouth when it was so foggy that we feared the game would be called off. This sea mist started rolling in and a Chelsea fan shouted, 'Jack The Ripper couldn't see in this fog!'

Richard Sharp

Extra-Time Goals Bring League Cup Success
To Vialli And Chelsea

Chelsea player-manager Gianluca Vialli yesterday brought the West London club another helping of Wembley glory and maintained the momentum that is gradually turning them into one of the leading forces in English football. He watched his side beat Middlesbrough 2-0 in the League Cup Final, with extra-time goals coming from Fank Sinclair and Roberta Di Matteo. Then, after the match was won, Dennis Wise, the Chelsea captain and man of the match, pushed his manager forward to walk up the Wembley steps to collect the trophy.

Oliver Holt, *The Times*, Monday 30th March 1998

Another Wembley Victory

Winning the League Cup in 1998 was good and brought back memories of the previous May, when we lifted the FA Cup. The players were really happy afterwards.

Jacquie Clarke

Not So Special

After the euphoria of winning the FA Cup, the League Cup Final wasn't really special. There was a cheer and everything when we lifted the trophy, but it wasn't that exciting.

Jamie Roberts

Ross Falconer takes the League Cup Final of 1998 in his stride, as the Chelsea Pensioners hurry to their seats.

AN ENGLISHMAN ABROAD

Although Chelsea's excursions into Europe can hardly be described as prolific, they have, in the main, been successful. Perhaps almost sensing that international opportunities would be few and far between, Chelsea have always grasped the bull firmly by the horns when faced with foreign opposition, and have been involved in some titanic encounters as a result. Domestic cup triumphs in 1970 and 1997 were both followed by European success the following season. Even Chelsea's venture in the European Cup Winners' Cup in 1994 had its moments, with the team reaching the semi-final stages of the competition. Here, we relive some of the best moments of those campaigns on foreign soil.

Hungary's Red Banner, playing at Stamford Bridge in the '50s.

Inter–City Fairs' Cup

In the 1965-66 season, Chelsea played AC Milan in the Inter-City Fairs' Cup. We had lost 2-1 over there and in the second leg at The Bridge, 60,000 turned up to see Chelsea win 2-1. Osgood scored a goal from about twenty-five yards that day.

We had to go and replay in Milan and ended up drawing 1-1. The tie was decided by flipping a coin, which we won. So Chelsea became the first British club to win in Italy and it was all down to the toss of a coin.

Kevin Ryan

European Glory

When Chelsea played in the European Cup Winners' Cup in 1971, the game finished 1-1 and went to a replay. The original match, against Real Madrid in Athens, wasn't shown on television. England were playing Wales that night and they showed the highlights of that match instead. So I listened to the first game on a crackling old radio that kept cutting out. I'd really wanted to go to Athens for the game but unfortunately I had a Spanish O-level examination the same day. As it happens, I passed the exam, so it was probably just as well I didn't go.

I watched the replay on TV from a pub in the King's Road, called the Stanley Arms. The place was packed. We were shoulder to shoulder and everyone was swaying. Nobody was drinking too much, they were just concentrating on the game. A huge cheer went up when the final whistle was blown. We'd beaten Real Madrid 2-1.

'Blue is the colour, Chelsea is our name!' – Dave Webb (front row, middle) leads the Song for Europe as the team celebrates Cup Winners' Cup success in '71.

After the original game the team had stayed out in Greece to prepare for the replay, forty-eight hours later. Of course, most of the fans had to come home. In fact, I spoke to a guy the other day who said, 'In 1971 I went to Athens – yet still ended up watching Chelsea win the cup from the King's Road!'

When the team arrived back on the Saturday, it was superb. Everyone stood outside the pubs in the King's Road and the place just erupted. It was about ten at night when the players got back and it was reported that at four in the morning, there were still five thousand fans in the streets celebrating. I remember going up to Trafalgar Square beforehand and seeing Chelsea fans dancing in the fountains. From there we went to the King's Road, where we stayed until the early hours. Then we started queuing up around the Town Hall for the official celebrations – we didn't bother going to bed. I think that I got home sometime around Monday night.

Andy Jackson

A Goal Rush

I'll never forget the time we defended the Cup Winner's Cup in 1972 against a Luxembourg team, Jeunesse Hautcharage. I think they had caused the all-time upset in Luxembourg by winning their cup from the Third Division. I don't even think this club had their own ground – they had to borrow one when they played us. They were really bad. It's not like today where the standard is generally okay at all levels – they were really dreadful. We beat them 8-0 away and when we played them at The Bridge we scored another thirteen goals. Three brothers played for them and, if my memory serves me right, one player had only one arm. I'm pretty sure that their centre-half played with his glasses tied on to his head. I'd never seen anyone play in glasses before, even at school. I was thirteen or fourteen at the time and I'd always thought it would be really great to see Chelsea smash someone. When it came to it, it was terrible. Dreadful – no contest at all. After the tenth goal it lost all its excitement.

Nigel Falconer

The Blue Army gathers in Czechoslovakia for the European Cup Winners' Cup game against Viktoria Zizkov in 1994.

The Cup Winners' Cup Campaigns Of The Nineties

In the 1994-95 season, despite finishing as only runners-up in the previous season's FA Cup competition, Chelsea represented England in the European Cup Winners' Cup. This was as a consequence of the FA Cup-winners, Manchester United, having also won the English Premier League, and thus taking up European commitments in the more prestigious Champions' League competition. Chelsea grasped this opportunity with both hands and headed straight into battle with Czechoslovakia's Viktoria Zizkov. The Blues easily overcame their first competitive European opponents in twenty-three years with a 4-2 aggregate score-line. Next on the agenda were Austria Memphis, who were a little more cumbersome to overpower, with Chelsea eventually going through on the away-goals rule thanks to a John Spencer strike in the away leg of the tie. Belgium's FC Bruges were the next team to be stopped in their tracks, before Chelsea finally succumbed to Spain's Zaragoza in the semi-final.

In the 1997-98 season, Chelsea went even further in the competition and lifted the trophy, defeating Germany's Stuttgart 1-0 in the final in Stockholm. The winning goal, from Gianfranco Zola, was the final step on the journey that had seen the Blues defeat Slovakia's Slovan Bratislava, Iceland's Tromso, Spain's Real Betis and Italy's Vicenza along the way.

Viktoria Zizkov

The first time we saw Chelsea in Europe was in 1994, against Czechoslovakian team Viktoria Zizkov. The police were worried about crowd trouble so the game wasn't played in Prague. Instead, they stuck us out on the Hungarian border. It was a great feeling to see Chelsea in a competitive game in Europe.

Nick Davis

Dennis Wise prepares for kick-off against Viktoria Zizkov, 1994.

Ghost Town

Zizkov was an afternoon kick-off. We were picked up at the airport and driven to the ground, thirty miles outside the town centre. We stopped off in the town first and found that nothing was open, save one bar. There was nowhere to go and the place was deserted. There weren't even any locals about. They'd obviously decided that they were being invaded by hooligans and creatures from outer space, and they didn't want to know about us.

Linda Richmond

Toilet Humour

We had a chartered flight and landed at Prague airport. There were four coaches waiting to take our plane load to the accommodation. We'd been warned by the trip organisers before we set off that we were to keep quiet, for fear of upsetting people. There was to be no singing or no drinking in the streets. Anyway, we got on our coach and the first thing that happened was that the driver stood up and asked, 'Do you like beer?' Everyone replied 'Yeah!', and he went to the hold and come back with a huge crate of lager. He charged us 20p a can. When we got to the game, it was just like being in an English non-league ground: tiny little stands and a bit of terracing. Behind the terrace was just woodland. One of the Chelsea fans asked a steward where the toilets were. The steward pointed to the woodland and said, 'Tree!' The supporter asked him, 'Which tree?', and he came back with, 'Any tree!'

Barry Jones

Armed Escort

The ground was unbelievably small. There are probably English Conference League clubs with better facilities. Only three sides of it were open and police with big dogs circled the whole thing. The Chelsea fans had a tiny standing section. They weren't selling programmes in our bit, so I went up to a policeman, smiled sweetly, and indicated that I wanted to buy a programme. The policeman gave me an armed escort to the programme seller in the home section. A programme cost about tuppence and all I had was their equivalent of about £1. I didn't care, so I just gave him the money and was escorted back. My friends and I had to share one programme between us.

Linda Richmond

Linda Richmond, Viktoria Zizkov, 1994.

Austria Memphis

My best moment in Europe was John Spencer's goal in Vienna, against Austria Memphis. In fact, that was the best football moment of my life. We'd drawn 0-0 at home in the second round and we had to score in Vienna to win. There was an hour gone and Memphis had a corner. Chelsea cleared the ball to Spencer, who was ten yards outside of his own area. He looked up and there were no Austrian players in sight. He ran the whole length of the pitch and scored. The 6,000 Chelsea fans went wild. I've never seen anything like it. They'd given us this section which normally held 12,000, so people were running up and down the aisles of empty seats in celebration. The look on the faces of the Austrian fans was something else. I mean, they like their football but they're not as passionate as we are, and they were just stunned. And when Memphis equalised, they just stood up and politely clapped for about ten seconds, before sitting down again.

Barry Jones

The Best Goal Ever

I swear that John Spencer ran faster with the ball than the Austrians could run without it. When Spencer put it away, I turned around and saw Matthew Harding dancing around the press box. I think that Spencer's strike was probably the best goal I've ever seen.

Andy Jackson

Little Legs

The atmosphere at the Austria Memphis game in Vienna was electric. Johnny Spencer was marvellous. He'd only just returned from injury. He's about the same height as me, five foot five, so to see his little legs run all the way from the half-way line to the opposing goal was amazing. And when he scored, it was just unbelievable. I still don't know how he got away from all the other players.

I was so washed out after that game that I hardly had the energy to celebrate. Before the game, the scenes were fantastic. When I checked-in at the airport to fly out, the North Terminal at Gatwick was packed solid with Chelsea fans. They were singing their hearts out. It was only seven in the morning but the place was a mass of blue and white, with scarves flying everywhere.

Fans gather in Slovakia for the European Cup Winners' Cup first round tie with Slovan Bratislava, 1997.

Linda Richmond

Bruges Away

When Chelsea played Bruges in the third round of the Cup Winners in 1995, there was this big fear about tickets falling into the hands of hooligans. Fans were strongly advised to buy the complete travelling package from Chelsea Football Club, to ensure they received a bona-fide ticket. Anyway, my girlfriend had an aunt who lived in Belgium. This aunt's boyfriend kindly travelled a hundred miles to Bruges and bought us some tickets for the home end.

We went over to Brussels the night before the match and then came down to Bruges on the morning of the game. The local newspapers stated that the police would arrest anyone speaking English in the 'wrong end'. Of course, we had these stupid Belgian tickets that didn't give any indication of where our seats were or which turnstiles to use. We got to the stadium really early, so that we could discreetly work out where we had to go. We also went respectfully dressed. I put on my work suit and my son hid away his colours. I even carried a letter from the guy who'd bought us the tickets, written in Belgian, saying that I was a respectable English businessman and not some hooligan.

We managed to get into the ground without speaking. This may all sound very silly, but there were huge numbers of people being arrested for no reason – just for speaking English. It was, 'Where do I go?', and bang, they were arrested. It was dreadful. I saw one guy in a wheelchair get arrested. I don't know what he was meant to have done. Nothing, I suppose. Just being English was enough.

Nigel Falconer

The Bratislava away leg, 1997. Chelsea won comfortably 2-0, with goals from Vialli and Di Matteo.

Bruges Supporters Club

The Bruges game was just after the infamous Ireland v England game, where the English fans had rioted. The authorities were a bit wary, to put it mildly. We stayed in Brussels and got a coach to Bruges fairly early in the day. It dropped us near to the ground and we started walking down the road to the turnstiles. We saw riot police, every now and again. They seemed to be grabbing passers by arbitrarily. I'd just had my hair cut short for the first time and I was worried that the police might think I was a hooligan. So we jumped into a bar, to wait until things outside had calmed down. It turned out to be hosting a Bruges supporters club meeting! We kept ourselves to ourselves, had a quiet beer and left.

Nick Davis

Clark Kent

We took our seats in the Bruges end. I knew that Bruges played in blue, white and red so I'd worn the nearest scarf I had to those colours. Then, all of a sudden, my son did this Clark Kent impression and pulled out his Chelsea scarf and banner. I couldn't believe it and was sure we were for it when the teams came out. The Belgians were singing this bloody monotonous one song over and over and were giving us nasty looks. Then the players arrived. The next thing I knew, the whole stand erupted in Chelsea chants and stood up to applaud our team. I couldn't believe my eyes: everyone around us was Chelsea incognito! How did these people get tickets, I wondered? It was a miracle that we'd got hold of any. Terrible game though. We lost 1-0.

Nigel Falconer

Chelsea take on Real Betis in the European Cup Winners' Cup third round, 1998.

Deported

Friends of mine travelled over to Belgium on the ferry. When they arrived, they asked where they had to go and were told, 'Stand over there.' They waited for hours and were then put on the first ferry out of the country. Deported, for no reason at all.

Barry Jones

A Friendly Match

A Chelsea supporters' club had arranged to play a friendly match before the game against Bruges' supporters. They had valid tickets for the match, but they were for the Bruges' end. They turned up to play their match and the police stopped them. They took one look at their tickets and were threatening to send them straight back to England. The Bruges' fans with them talked the police round and they calmed things down. The police were dreadful that day.

Nick Davis

Real Zaragoza

When we lost 3-0 to Real Zaragoza in the semi-final of the Cup Winners' Cup in 1995, I paid £275 to fly out there for the day and the plane was still delayed. We ended up having just four hours in Zaragoza, including the match, before flying home.

As the coach pulled into the town before the game, I noticed these urchin-type kids by the side of the road. They were gazing at the Chelsea coaches coming through and they were all holding up three fingers to predict the score-line. They ended up being right – I don't know how they knew!

The Spanish police herded the Chelsea supporters into this one square. In the cafes, the price of lager kept going up and up as more Chelsea supporters arrived. We managed to break away and go round a few local bars. We spoke to a few Spanish fans and they were really friendly. Inside the ground it was a horrible atmosphere, with the police sitting watching, with their batons. We were quite near the Spanish fans and they kept making nasty gestures. A strange thing that struck me was the size of the Spanish police horses. They were tiny – more like ponies. Another strange thing occurred to me in the first-half, when a shot just skimmed our bar. Whereas excited English fans would go 'Ooooooh!', the Spanish fans went 'Eyeeeeee!' 35,000 people going 'Eyeeeeee!' seemed really comical.

Richard Sharp

A Fun Day Regardless

Zaragoza was a bit odd. It was quite a good day out even though we lost. The plane was delayed but it didn't seem to matter. We got there, sneaked through the police cordon and had a drink with the home fans – it was fun.

We got into the ground and we started up 'Glenn Hoddle's blue and white army!' for about twenty minutes. After five minutes, my throat gave up. We got stuffed that day. It was 3-0, and a real 3-0 at that. Not even close.

Ron Coello

Cough Mixture And Lager

I went to Zaragoza full of flu! The police wouldn't allow us to walk anywhere in the town so we just stood in this square drinking. By the time it came to kick-off, I was high on a mixture of Night Nurse, Benolin and lager! The game was terrible. We lost 3-0 and we were lucky to get nil that day.

Tony Sharp

Right: The Red Lion 'watering hole', Costa Del Sol, as visited by Barry Jones and countless other Blues fans en route to Seville.

Beat Betis!

We went to the Real Betis game in Spain in the 1997-98 season. That trip was great. We made a real holiday of it, spending a few days in the Costa Del Sol before moving on to Seville for the match. We met a lot of Seville fans before the game. They're big rivals of Real Betis and kept coming up and saying, 'Beat Betis! Beat Betis!' I saw a kid in a Betis strip who was trying to swap shirts with passing Chelsea fans. No chance of that – not at £40 a throw for a Chelsea shirt.

Barry Jones

The historic city of Seville, home to Real Betis.

Friendly Opposition

For the Real Betis match, we could only get tickets for the non-Chelsea seats. The club and the police were aware of this and advised us not to go into home fan sections. We thought we'd try our luck anyway. We got in there and there was no bother at all. The Betis supporters were superb.

Nick Davis

Mulder And Scully

I knew that Chelsea would beat Vicenza in the European Cup Winners' Cup semi-final in 1998, at Stamford Bridge. It didn't matter that Chelsea had lost the first leg 1-0. It didn't even matter that we'd recently parted company with our manager, Ruud Gullit. I knew that Chelsea couldn't lose because the hand of fate was on our side and I'd been given 'a sign'.

On the Saturday before the game, I was standing in the kitchen, sorting through the post. My wife was making breakfast. Just at the point I opened the envelope from the club containing our tickets for the Vicenza game, my wife poured the Sugar Puffs into a cereal bowl. What should fall out of the cereal packet but a blue, plastic Graeme Le Saux pencil topper! We both looked at each other, before I said, 'That's a sure sign. Our name's on the cup.' Some people might say that I'm being a bit over the top here, but they weren't in the kitchen that day. I nearly called for Mulder and Scully!

Nick Hines

Graeme Le Saux – Novelty pencil topper and ace footballer.

Stockholm '98

The 1998 European Cup Winners' Cup Final in Stockholm was a little different for me to most fans. I come from Stuttgart and they are my boyhood team. I now live in London, however, and support Chelsea. So I was supporting both competing finalists. From the outset I said, 'I can't lose!'. I never said, 'I can't win!' My heart was sixty-forty in favour of Stuttgart, but when Chelsea won, I was still very happy for them. I'm sure that I was one of the last people to leave the Stuttgart end. The other German supporters didn't hang around for the Chelsea celebrations.

I wore a joint Stuttgart-Chelsea scarf to the game. It's a lovely souvenir from such a special occasion.

Jochen Staudt

Jochen Staudt, Stockholm, 1998.

A Marvellous Day

Stockholm was a marvellous occasion. I've spoken to people who watched on TV at home and they've told me what a let-down it was. Well, if these people had been there and experienced the tension, the drama and the excitement, they'd have a different opinion, I'm sure.

I got to Stockholm at eight in the morning and the whole day was marvellous. The sun shone, it was a beautiful city and the people were lovely. I constantly saw Chelsea and German fans mingling and everything was really friendly.

Scott Cheshire

Carefree

We found this nice bar in Stockholm. It was really quite posh. They allowed Chelsea fans in, but we weren't allowed to sing, for fear of upsetting the other drinkers. Every now and then the chant would go up, 'Carefree, wherever you may be, we are the famous CFC … ', and the waiter would come over and very politely ask us to quieten down. We'd oblige and then half an hour later, the singing would start again.

Daryl Woodward

Chelsea fans sample Swedish hospitality before the European Cup Winners' Cup Final in Stockholm, 1998.

Peter Osgood

We couldn't have had a better day. We walked all around Stockholm, had a nice lunch and saw all the supporters swapping shirts. We even saw Peter Osgood sitting outside a cafe having a glass of wine and enjoying the atmosphere.

We got back to England in the early hours and found ourselves back at home watching the video of the game at six o'clock in the morning.

Jan Bettis

Thunderbirds

We went to Stockholm on a coach package, which included three ferry crossings and an overnight stay in Gothenburg. The whole day was fantastic. As we got close to the ground, the coach driver asked us if we could quieten down the singing because we had company! We looked out of the window and saw Swedish police motor cyclists following us. They stopped the coach and one of them got onboard. He looked liked a Thunderbird puppet with his little hat and his knee-length boots. He said, 'Welcome everybody. I've got maps here for you all, showing you where the places of interest are. Enjoy your stay!'

On the way home we got the coach driver to play the song 'Blue Day' so many times, that by the end of the journey he knew the words off by heart.

Jacquie Clarke

Pre-match ceremony at the Cup Winners' Cup Final, Stockholm.

All In Blue

The whole day in Stockholm was fantastic. We met at the airport at four in the morning and within no time, everyone was standing on the seats and singing. Johnnie Vaughan from Channel Four's *The Big Breakfast* arrived and a Chelsea fan rugby-tackled him.

When we arrived in Stockholm, there was blue everywhere. As for in the stadium – well, we really were a blue army. I'd made a special effort for the occasion, dying my hair blue and donning blue sunglasses.

When Zola scored our winner, everyone went mental. I was sitting in row fifty but ended up falling into row twenty. I remember rolling down over the seats. Everyone was hugging each other. It was fantastic.

It was really expensive to go to the Cup Winners' Cup Final. I didn't mind forking out because I'd given myself a choice: I'd decided to either go watch England in the World Cup, or travel out to Stockholm. It wasn't really a difficult choice, to be honest.

Jamie Roberts

Invasion '98 – The Blue Army arrives in Stockholm.

Turning the town blue – West London moves to Sweden.

Dambusters

The whole day was really relaxed. De Ghoey in goal was great, as he had been in the whole competition. He definitely won us the cup.

The Stuttgart fans were great. Before the game, you'd see them coming towards you and the Chelsea fans would start humming The Dambusters' theme! They'd start laughing, you'd start laughing, and you'd end up shaking hands and wishing each other luck. It was really nice.

I was standing in a bar before the game and I went to get something out of my pocket. I tried to hold my beer glass in my mouth and managed to pull out my front crown. I had to watch the whole game with a stump where my crown used to be. I was lisping, 'Come on Chelsea!' The day cost me quite a lot: £350 on travel and tickets, £40 on lager and £200 to have my tooth fixed! A perfect day out!

Tony Sharp

Jacquie Clarke and family, in Stockholm for the European Cup Winners' Cup Final, 1998.

FEELING BLUE

Good times, bad times, they come and go, but one thing remains: an allegiance to the cause of them all. Elation one minute and then heartbreak the next – the devout Chelsea fan has become accustomed to fluctuating emotions over the years. But as one supporter said earlier, 'You can change your house, your job, even your wife … but not your team!' Once you've made that decision to follow Chelsea, you're stuck with them through thick and thin, and, whatever state of mind they put you in, it's a safe bet that you'll be 'feeling blue' for the rest of your days.

Roy Coello and son, Peter, having a 'blue moment'.

An Irrational Hatred

It's amazing how passionate I can get over football. At the weekend I went to a party and I started making fun of a few Arsenal fans, just for the sake of it. They responded in their usual Arsenal superior style. I hate Arsenal, but without good reason – it's a very irrational hatred. Tom Watt, a very good friend of mine, is very passionate about Arsenal. There's nothing I like better than ringing up his telephone answer-machine and leaving a message when we've beaten them.

Andy Jacobs

den Bros.]

THE CHELSEA ELEVEN IN THE NORTHERN GOAL AT STAMFORD BRIDGE.

WATSON. McROBERTS. KEY.   WINDRIDGE. MACKIE. { FOULKE, } COPELAND. J. T. ROBERTSON. McEWAN. MORAN. KIRWAN.
{ Captain. }

From where the passion stems – The Chelsea team of 1905 prepare to take on the world.

Friday, Saturday, Sunday

Football can take over your life. Friday you do nothing but think about it because you're looking forward to the game. Saturday revolves around that one and a half hours in the middle. Then come Sunday, you're generally fed up from it all and want an early night.

Ron Coello

The Chelsea Postman

One day I was getting into the car when the postman went past and asked, 'Are you a Chelsea season ticket holder?' I said, 'Yes, how did you guess?' He answered, 'I've been delivering your Chelsea magazine, *Onside*, all year.' Anyway, I didn't think anything more about it until one day I got a card through the door saying that he'd tried to deliver a parcel when I was out. On the back of the card he'd written, 'Come on you Blues!' I went up to the depot to pick up the parcel a few days later. The bloke behind the window looked at the card and said, 'You must have 'Nutty' delivering your mail!'

I've seen him at Stamford Bridge since then and he's told me that he's not doing my postal round anymore. He told me not to worry, though, because my new postman is 'Chelsea' too.

Tony Sharp

Right: Blues supporters in the streets of Seville for the 1998 European Cup Winners' Cup tie with Spain's Real Betis.

A Clash Of Interests

When me and the missus had been going out for a while, she said, 'If we're going to get married, we should set a date soon.' I responded, 'Fair enough,' and left the organising to her. Later, she came back to me with a suggested date in August. I took one look at it and said, 'Hang on, it's the first game of the season!' She got really annoyed and stormed off. I pointed out that if Chelsea were playing, none of 'the boys' would come along to the wedding. Even I wouldn't turn up. She eventually came round and we brought the wedding forward a week. We had a lovely ceremony, a couple of days honeymoon, and got to see the first game of the season after all.

Nick Davis

Hero

I've taken my wife to Stamford Bridge only once, over fifteen years ago. We were playing Newcastle and Kevin Keegan was in their team. I think she was quite shocked at the abuse thrown at him. She'd thought we'd treat him like a national hero.

Paul Fisher

Where's The Goalie's Hair?

Chelsea always applaud the away 'keeper when he approaches the goal at the start of each half. David Seaman always gets a good clap because he plays for England. Then someone reminds him of Arsenal's Cup Winners' Cup defeat by singing, 'Nayim from the half-way line!'

Making fun of away 'keepers is always good. I remember once when Chelsea went up to Manchester City and we had a go at Joe Corrigan. We were singing, 'Corrigan, Corrigan, where's your hair?' He just patted his head and turned round and shrugged at us. Of course, after that, we cheered everything he did. At one point, we even sang, 'We love you Joey, we do!'

Richard Sharp

Bob Marley For Chelsea!

Before I go to a big game, I carry out a bizarre ritual. I always play Bob Marley's 'Waiting In Vain'. We played Sheffield Wednesday years ago in the cup and it went to extra-time. In the gap between full-time and extra-time, the club played that song and I said, 'Boys, we're going to win this!' And we did, so I always play it on important match-days now. Unfortunately, the magic was destroyed when we lost 5-3 to Man United.

Ron Coello

Clean Hair, Nice Shirt

Before every home game I do the same thing: I wash my hair first thing in the morning and put on the same sweatshirt. I'll keep doing this until we're defeated – then that'll be another ritual up in smoke.

Paul Fisher

The one 'keeper no one dared make fun of – Willie Foulke keeps goal for Chelsea, early 1900s.

Lucky Red Jeans

For the successful FA Cup-run in 1997, I wore a yellow Chelsea T-shirt to every game. I was on holiday the following year, and I saw these red jeans. I thought, 'They could be my lucky jeans!' So I bought them, and I wore them to every European Cup Winners' Cup game. I didn't go to the Tromso game, so my jeans couldn't travel and we lost. But apart from that, my red jeans were unbeaten.

Nick Davis

Blues supporters Chris Crighton and Neil Beard sample local hospitality, during the half-time interval in the European Cup Winners' Cup match with Slovan Bratislava, 1997.

Score Draw

If anyone ever needs a guaranteed score draw for the pools, just pay for me and my daughter to go to a match. The first game I took her to was Chelsea versus Sheffield Wednesday. We dominated the game and were winning 1-0. Then two minutes from the end, Sheffield scored on their one raid. At half-time she was bored and said, 'I want to go home, Daddy.' She was five at the time.

I took her again, the year after, when Chelsea played Newcastle in the cup. A defensive lapse by our 'keeper, Kharine, in the last few minutes gave Les Ferdinand the equaliser. The game ended 1-1. The next game I took her to was against Wimbledon. That ended 1-1. So if anyone requires three points on their pools coupon, my daughter is available at very reasonable rates.

Peter Scherschel

Place Your Bets

When my daughter was born, I left my wife in hospital to go and see Chelsea play at home. I was bang out of order, I admit. My little girl knows how much I like football now. If we pass a football ground, she goes, 'Football! That's where Daddy lives!'

My little girl's called Katie. A lot of people lost money on that one. There were a lot of bets placed on me calling her 'Chelsea'.

Nick Davis

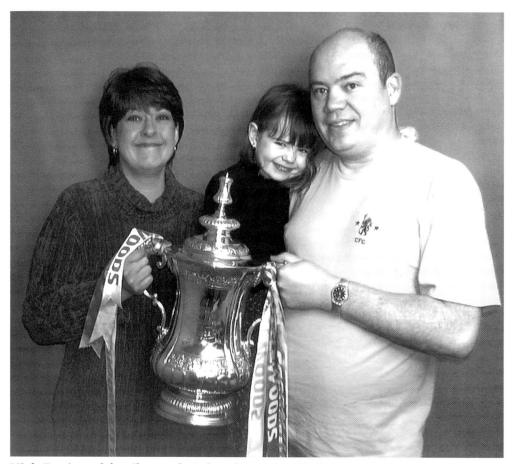

Nick Davis and family get their hands on the FA Cup.

A Mad Obsession

My son, Alexander, is three-and-a-half and he already knows what football's all about. From the age of one, he knew who Ruud Gullit was. My girlfriend was travelling on a bus once and a guy with dreadlocks got on. My son started shouting, 'Rudi! Rudi! Rudi!' I found that really funny. I quite like that mad obsession with football.

Actually, my girlfriend thinks I'm obsessed with Chelsea. Not with football, but with Chelsea.

Ron Coello

Baby Blues

The first time I took my son to Stamford Bridge he was only eighteen-months-old. It was a play-off game against Blackburn. I think we won 4-0. It might seem young, but I think it's important.

Nigel Falconer

Right: Nigel Falconer and son Ross, on their way to the League Cup Final of 1998.

A Vow Of Silence

There was a game against Chelsea when we were losing 1-0 and I had been moaning about our performance for the whole of the first half. I'd been moaning so much that I even got on my own nerves. I thought, 'This is counterproductive – what am I doing?' So I made a decision not to speak for the whole second half. It was a new policy: shut up and watch the game. And it was very interesting because as soon as I shut up, my kids started shouting and complaining. They were compensating for me.

Andy Jacobs

Left: Chelsea memorabilia from the '50s.

A Change Of Seats

Last year we moved seats to the Matthew Harding Upper Stand. Unfortunately though, with this stand you don't get the chance to choose where you sit. You just apply in the close season and get put on a list with other would-be ticket holders. It's the luck of the draw as to which seats you're given. So I wrote this really pathetic letter to accompany my application. I said that I went to games with two short people and that it was really important that we got a good view. The next thing I knew, one of the Stamford Bridge general managers rang me at work and asked, 'Is the front row okay?' Cool as I could be I replied, 'Yeah, that should be fine.' I was terrified the club would send me and my family for a medical, though.

Nigel Falconer

Jack's Black Book

In the 1970s, there was always a great rivalry with Leeds. Jack Charlton apparently had a black book which he used to log the names of players he was going to settle a score with. I'm pretty sure that Peter Osgood was in it. There was no quarter given in games with Leeds. Looking back at footage of those matches, some of the tackles seem really brutal.

Jim McSweeney

Peter Osgood in the '90s - Probably still in Jack Charlton's 'Black Book'.

Albert Bridge

In 1968 when Manchester United won the European Cup, all the kids where I lived supported them. I could never understand that. Why live in London and support United? I support Chelsea because I was brought up in Battersea and could walk to the ground. My dad supported them before me, so we just went to The Bridge, without question.

I remember going over Albert Bridge with my dad for the first time and seeing all the houseboats that had been in trendy '60's films. It seemed a really glamorous place to be. Now, with all the foreign players coming to the club, Chelsea is becoming really glamorous again.

Nigel Falconer

Chelsea In Bangkok

Chelsea played the Thai national side in a pre-season friendly in 1997. I live in Singapore and managed to go over to Bangkok for a few days and watch the game. I sat in the 1500 baht seats and the view was okay. I was under cover and sheltered from the sun. It did seem expensive though, paying the equivalent of £37.50 to see Chelsea win a friendly 1-0. Especially when you consider that my '97 Cup Final ticket was only £17.

Away to my right, basking in the sunshine, was a group of twenty to thirty Chelsea fans who looked like they'd made the trip from the UK. They seemed in very high spirits, singing and waving flags. The atmosphere was great. The crowd started a Mexican wave after fifteen minutes and even the Chelsea bench joined in, to the delight of the fans.

Outside the ground I met up with the Thai Chelsea Supporters group and had a little chat. They were all very excited about the game and the FA Cup win. One of them even had the new CFC logo painted on the bonnet of his car.

Eventually the crowd of 30,000 melted away into the streets of Bangkok. We fought our way into a taxi and headed back to the hotel for triple the normal fare.

Stephen Fairclough

It's a long way home – Chelsea fans wait in an airport departure lounge after a European excursion.

A Boro Fan Speaks

The only time I've been to Stamford Bridge was in the 1995-96 season. I went with my mate Paul, who is a Middlesbrough supporter, to see Chelsea put five past Boro.

I don't remember much about the game, except that every time Chelsea attacked, they scored. The atmosphere in the away supporters end was great. Even at 5-0 down! The Chelsea fans were singing, 'We want six! We want six!', and the Boro started up, 'We want one! We want one!' Then the Chelsea started, 'Can we play you every week?'

I also remember that Gullit came on as a substitute and got a great reception from the Middlesbrough supporters. The bloke next to me said that Gullit was still different class and he was right. I remember being taken aback at how big he was. He was a giant of a man, very impressive, with a huge presence.

Nick Bennett

The scourge of Middlesbrough – That man Di Matteo, leaving the pitch after the European tie with Real Betis, 1998.

A Special Gift

Why do I support Chelsea? Well, I suppose it's because one of my earliest memories is of receiving a Chelsea kit in a big rectangular box, when I was three or four. It was bought for me by my grandfather. He wasn't a Chelsea fan himself but picked that kit because Chelsea were one of the big teams around at the time.

Daryl Woodward

Dad Knows Best

My dad bought me a Chelsea kit when I was four. I'm a bit embarrassed to admit it, but I actually wanted a West Ham kit. I remember my dad putting me right, saying, 'No, son, Chelsea are the best side. You'll find this out in a few years when I start taking you.' From that day on it's been Chelsea, Chelsea, Chelsea!

Jamie Roberts

Supporter Paul Day models the 1998-99 away strip.

Jamie Roberts.

Good Times All Round

I've only been going to Stamford Bridge since 1994, so I've seen quite a few highs and not many lows. My boyfriend and his son have been going for years and talk about this game or that game when we lost 2-0 and they got soaked in the rain – but I've never really experienced any bad times. I mean, in the short time I've been going I've seen us win the FA Cup, League Cup, and Cup Winners' Cup. When Chelsea eventually win the championship, I might have to pick another team to support. They'll have peaked and it'll be all downhill from then on.

Jan Bettis

Right: Jan Bettis enjoys Chelsea's defeat of Middlesbrough in the League Cup Final of 1998.

Guillit Is A Fairy!

The first time we had a real Christmas tree, we decided that it would be too boring to cover it in tinsel, so we got lots of old programmes and cut them up, and decorated the tree in Chelsea players. The fairy on the top was Ruud Gullit! That's pretty sad, isn't it? But it did look really good.

Sue Hawkins

Chelsea Ladies

Jacquie Clarke (right) and Louise Bundick turn out for the Blues in 1976.

In the mid 1970s I played for the Supporters Club Ladies team and we were trained by a couple of players on a Friday night. Ray Lewington and Teddy Maybank would normally train us. We had all the normal kit. We also had these special sweatshirts with 'Chelsea Supporters Ladies FC' on them, which we wore to five-a-side matches. I didn't have my name on the back though.

I played in defence. My equivalent player in the first team would have been Graham Wilkins. I was probably a touch better than him.

Jacquie Clarke

Blue Christmas

Just after the Second World War, Chelsea used to play on Christmas Day. One year, me and a friend walked from Battersea over to Chelsea for an eleven o'clock kick-off. We got there at half eight in the morning. We were standing by the main gates when the Gatekeeper came out and asked what we were doing in the freezing cold. We said that we had come to watch Chelsea and he said, 'Well, you can't stand out here. Follow me.' He took us into his hut and gave us hot tea and biscuits. While we were in there, the opposing team's coach turned up. The players came in and started talking to us. Me and my friend were mesmerised. They gave us tickets for the Main Stand and we ended up watching the game from the best seats, overlooking the bench.

Stan Falconer

Right: James Argue - Signed in the 1933-34 season, Argue went on to be a great servant to Chelsea and was a member of the first post-war team of 1946.

Brotherly Love

I remember coming out of West Ham once with my brother and getting on to a tube train. We got seats opposite a really attractive girl. My brother's not a bad looking bloke and this girl clearly took a shine to him. She saw the crowds and started up a conversation. She asked what was going on. My brother told her that there had been a football match. She said, 'Did you win?' and I answered, 'Yes, we won 2-1.' I suddenly noticed that the carriage was full of West Ham supporters staring at me. I corrected myself, 'Errr, no! We lost!' My brother was punching me in the leg.

Richard Sharp

Beefy In The Loo!

I met Ian Botham once, in the toilets at Sheffield Wednesday. It was just after Chelsea had brought out this magazine called *Bridge News*. In the first or second issue, there was a picture of a subscription cheque made out by Ian and Kathy Botham. Apparently, he was a big Chelsea fan. So anyway, we were playing at Sheff Wed and at half-time I went to the loo and found myself standing next to Botham. So I said to him, 'I hope your cheque for *Bridge News* didn't bounce!' He turned around and, well, I've never seen anyone look so angry in their life. He snarled at me and I just zipped up my flies and ran out the toilet. No sense of humour at all, that bloke.

Barry Jones

Stamford The Lion meets the mascot of the day.

Mac Attack

On the way back from an away game once, the coach stopped at a service station. We piled into the cafe and noticed the Manchester City player with the long hair, Paul Walsh, eating a Big Mac. It was a shock – footballers don't eat junk food! He got loads of stick. Everyone who had been to an away match that day was congregating there and having a go at him. So when I heard that Arsenal's Paul Merson had taken cocaine, I wasn't particularly shocked. I'd already seen a pro' eating a burger.

Nigel Falconer

Sign Here Please

A couple of years a go, a friend of mine was very seriously ill. I wrote to Chelsea saying that my mate was a season ticket holder and that he couldn't get to the matches easily because of his illness. I got a telephone call from Ken Bates' secretary saying that the club had reserved a car-parking space and two tickets for the Directors' Box for the forthcoming game against Blackburn.

We went to the match and in the bar beforehand we met Matthew Harding and his dad. Matthew signed my programme. Later, in the toilets, I bumped into Jack Walker, the Blackburn chairman. He signed my programme too. Considering how rich these two men were, I reckon I must own the most expensive programme in the world.

Kevin Ryan

Kevin Ryan (centre) with friends on a European excursion.

Tony The Train Driver

I started supporting Chelsea through a friend from work. When I first started going and met his football mates, it struck me as really funny that they all had nicknames. There was Big Tones, Rick The Geezer and even a bloke going by the name of Captain Wayne. He had been on the television game show *The Crystal Maze* and had been captain of one of the teams – thus the nickname. All the names seemed to have some strange derivation. None of them had anything to do with Chelsea, other than that they were only used on match days. The funniest name, to me, was that of Tony The Train Driver. I could never work why the others called him that and it was years before I eventually found out. Apparently, he was called Tony and drove a train for a living. Maybe I was thinking a bit too deeply about that one.

Nick Hines

The author in artistic football pose.

Moments Of Pleasure

The rare moments of pleasure Chelsea give me make all the heartache worthwhile. When you taste success only now and then, it makes it all the sweeter. I did say to someone years ago, that if we won the cup I wouldn't want us to win anything ever again. But now, I want us to win something every season. But if we never have any more success, at least I've seen some great games and spent time with people I enjoy being with. Football has formed quite an important part of my life in that way and it's very dear to me. It's difficult to explain to someone who doesn't like football what these feelings are like. There have been moments when I've thought to myself, 'I just can't beat this feeling' – those times when I'm in a pub with my friends and I've just seen Chelsea win a great game. Fantastic times.

Ron Coello